AN INTRODUCTION TO
PICTURE
FRAMING

AN INTRODUCTION TO
PICTURE
FRAMING

VIVIEN FRANK

CHARTWELL
BOOKS, INC.

A QUINTET BOOK

Published by Chartwell Books
A Division of Book Sales, Inc.
110 Enterprise Avenue
Secaucus, New Jersey 07094

ISBN 1-55521-581-5

This book was designed and produced by
Quintet Publishing Limited
6 Blundell Street
London N7 9BH

Creative Director: Peter Bridgewater
Art Director: Ian Hunt
Designer: James Lawrence
Illustrator: Danny McBride
Project Editors: Judith Simons and
Henrietta Wilkinson
Editor: Betty Floyd
Photographer: Ian Howes

Typeset in Great Britain by
Central Southern Typesetters, Eastbourne
Manufactured in Hong Kong by
Regent Publishing Services Limited
Printed in Hong Kong
by Kwong Fat Offset Printing Company Limited

CONTENTS

INTRODUCTION **6**

TOOLS & EQUIPMENT **7**

LIGHTWEIGHT FRAMES **17**

MAT BOARD FRAMES **27**

CLAY & PAPIER-MACHE FRAMES **51**

CUTOUT FRAMES **61**

WOODEN FRAMES **71**

FABRIC FRAMES **85**

MULTIPLE FRAMES **97**

BOX FRAMES **105**

READY-MADE FRAMES **115**

APPENDIX **121**

INTRODUCTION

There are many different ways to frame a picture. This book shows you how to achieve decorative, stylish and pleasing effects without spending a vast amount of money at a framer's shop.

Certain pictures, such as old masters and other valuable works, are best left to the professional framer, and some decorative techniques, such as gilding, are so specialized that they are outside the scope of this book. But there are still numerous picture framing techniques that an interested and creative person can easily undertake.

A frame plays a major role in the total visual impact of the artwork it surrounds – it can enhance or detract. For this reason, you should take great care in selecting materials. The choice of materials is subjective; in general, it is governed more by taste than by rules. If possible, look around friends' homes, art galleries and museums for styles, ideas and current fashions.

The frame isolates the picture from its surroundings and gives it importance. But it should also act as a bridge relating the work to those surroundings and to its general environment. It is important, therefore, to find a balance; this usually involves achieving the right proportions – a skill that will come with experience.

The techniques used throughout the book are easily mastered, and the equipment and materials required need not be expensive. You can, for example, give a child's painting importance by framing it with a mat created to complement it; you can make a decorative frame using fabric to match the decor of a room; or you can enhance a special photograph with a simple wooden cutout frame. This book is designed to dispel some of the mystique surrounding the interesting craft of framemaking and to encourage readers to enjoy creating a variety of frames. A little patience and preparation is all you need to design and create professional-looking picture frames.

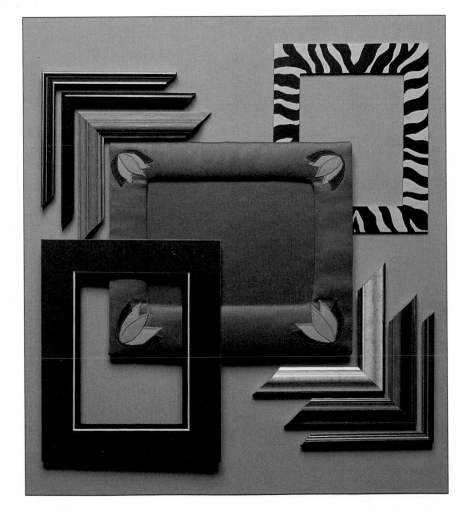

TOOLS AND EQUIPMENT

PAPER AND CARD MATS **8**

TRADITIONAL MOLDINGS **10**

MODERN MOLDINGS **11**

TOOLS **12**

EQUIPMENT **14**

ACCESSORIES **16**

PAPER AND CARD MATS

1 (from left to right) Smooth-surface hardboard, standard hardboard, acid-free backing card, gray backing card.

2 Assorted papers including watercolor paper and textured paper.

3 Standard matting, including acid-free, conservation quality and black core.

4 Matting with textured surfaces, for example, Ingres, linen, flecked and fabric.

TRADITIONAL MOLDINGS

■ A selection of traditional style moldings, with gold and natural wood finishes predominating.

MODERN MOLDINGS

A selection of modern style moldings. The moldings themselves are quite plain in comparison with traditional styles, but are available in a wide range of colors and finishes.

TOOLS

1 miter box
2 tenon saw
3 miter clamp
4 frame clamp
5 try square
6 hand plane
7 drill bits
8 glass cutter
9 nail set/nail punch
10 tack hammer
11 pliers
12 small screwdriver
13 bradawl
14 multi-screwdriver

3

4

5

6

7

8

9

10

11

EQUIPMENT

1 double-side clear adhesive tape
2 gummed tape
3 self-adhesive tape
4 plastic ruler
5 mat cutter with integral ruler
6 corner gauge
7 mat cutter
8 scissors
9 circle cutter
10 paint
11 pencil
12 paint brushes
13 wax pencil
14 assorted felt-tip pens
15 compass
16 craft knife
17 metal triangle
18 glue pen
19 cutting mat

4

5

7

6

LONGRIDGE
CORNER GAUGE

PATENT FOR
APPLIED

8

9

15

11

12

14

13

10

1 plastic self-adhesive
    hangers
2 tacks
3 brass picture wire
4 easel hinges
5 clips for "frameless"
    frames
6 various sizes of
    screw eyes
7 D-rings
8 screw rings
9 triangle hangers
10 rings and clips
11 rivets for D-rings
12 glaziers' points
13 turn clips
14 mirror clips
15 metal center
    hangers
16 frame stand
17 plastic-coated
    picture wire
18 gummed hangers

LIGHTWEIGHT FRAMES

CARDS WITH SLITS **18**

SIMPLE CUTOUT FRAME **19**

FOLDED CARD FRAMES **20**

DECORATED FOLDED FRAMES **22**

ORIGAMI PICTURE FRAMES **24**

FOLDED CORNERS AND BACKING **26**

CARDS WITH SLITS

This is a simple way to frame a picture or photograph. If done with care, it can produce a surprisingly effective look.

EQUIPMENT

- pencil
- ruler
- craft knife or scalpel
- paper or lightweight card

VARIATION 1

To enhance the picture, choose card for the frame in a color that complements it. Take extra care in deciding on the width of the surround as this will also affect the final look. For a small picture about the size of a postcard, you can incorporate an easel in the frame to make it free-standing (see page 48).

1 Decide on the overall size of the frame, mark the dimensions on a piece of card and cut out. Draw faint lines to show the position of the picture and then mark the corners symmetrically, as shown in Fig. 1, to show where the slits will be. Cut the slits.

2 If using an easel to make this frame free-standing, follow Fig. 1 on page 48. After scoring, fix in position.

3 Carefully insert the corners of the picture into the slits in the frame.

VARIATION 2

Another simple card frame with slits is shown in Fig. 2. Here the slits are less evident; they also provide more support for a larger picture.

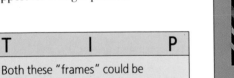

TIP

Both these "frames" could be decorated using one of the methods explained later in this chapter or in the section dealing with mat decoration in the next chapter.

1 Again, take care in selecting the color of the card for the frame.

2 Using the diagram in Fig. 2, prepare and cut two slits in each corner.

3 A gummed hook fixed to the center back of the card is used to display the completed frame – this is suitable for lightweight frames only.

4 Insert each corner of the picture in one slit and out of the other. The two slits provide a band across each corner to hold the picture firmly.

SIMPLE CUT-OUT FRAME

This is a more decorative but equally straightforward way to frame a small picture.

EQUIPMENT

- as previous project
- acetate (optional)
- elastic bands
- thin dowel
- hole punch

3 This frame can be displayed in a variety of ways – free-standing, with gummed hangers or with an easel.

PREPARATION

Cut out two pieces of card to the required dimensions for the frame. Decide on the width of the surround and cut a window in one piece. Attach the picture to the other piece and place the piece with the window cut-out on top. Acetate can be placed over the "frame".

1 Punch two holes at the top and two at the bottom (see Fig. 3).

2 Cut two pieces of dowel the width of the card. Thread an elastic band through the two top holes and around the ends of one dowel. Repeat through the other two holes and around the ends of the other dowel – this secures the frame.

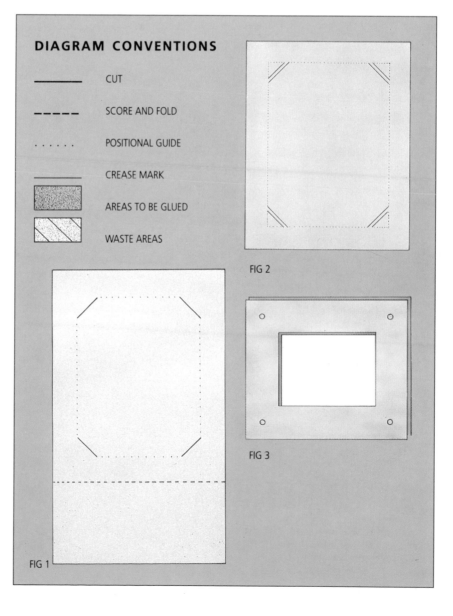

DIAGRAM CONVENTIONS

———	CUT
– – –	SCORE AND FOLD
· · · · ·	POSITIONAL GUIDE
———	CREASE MARK
▓▓▓	AREAS TO BE GLUED
▨▨▨	WASTE AREAS

FIG 2

FIG 1

FIG 3

FOLDED CARD FRAMES

VARIATION 1

This technique is often used to frame photographs which are to be sent by mail. The frame is made from a single fold of card.

As with all frames, choose your materials carefully. If the finished frame is to be mailed, consider the size of readily available envelopes when planning the project.

EQUIPMENT

- pencil
- ruler
- craft knife or scalpel
- paper or lightweight card

1 Cut the card to the required size and lightly mark the center. Lay the ruler along this line and score with the back of the knife or a bone folder, taking care not to cut through the card.

2 Fold the card along the crease mark and secure the picture in position using either the slits method shown on the previous page or with invisible photo-mounts or photo-corners.

3 The frame protects the photograph in the mail and can also be used as a stand.

VARIATION 2

A simple folded card frame can be embellished to make a more decorative frame. Examples are shown on the following pages. This frame has an extra fold so the photograph is completely enclosed.

EQUIPMENT

- as previous project
- piece of white paper
- scissors
- photo-mounts

PREPARATION

- The basic method can be adapted. Decide on the overall dimensions of the frame. This frame was designed to fit a standard envelope – its dimensions, when folded, are ¼in (0.5cm) smaller in both length and width than the envelope.
- The piece of card from which the frame was made was 6in × 12¾in (15.5cm × 33cm) – that is, the same length as the folded card and three times the width. Score the card so that it is divided into three equal parts.

1 In this frame, the photograph is displayed through an oval opening. To make the oval, start with a piece of thin, white paper the same size as one of the three sections of the frame and fold it into quarters. Decide on the height and width of the opening and mark half of each of these measurements on the piece of paper (see Fig. 1).

2 Draw a curve to join the two marks (see Fig. 2). Then cut along the line and unfold the paper – an oval has been created (see Fig. 3). If the shape is not pleasing, try again.

3 Position the oval cutout in the required position on the middle third of the piece of card (see Fig. 4). Draw around the oval.

4 Carefully cut the oval out.

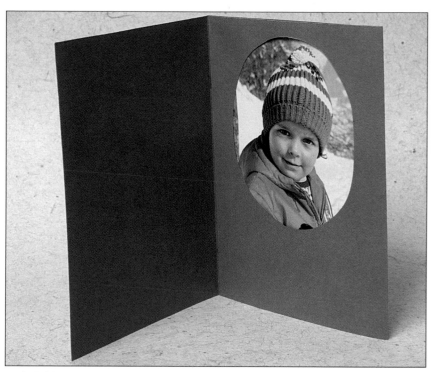

5 Place the photograph in position on the reverse side of the righthand third of the card and stick in place with photo-mounts, so that the photograph shows through the window. Then stick this to the center section.

6 The lefthand third of the card can be folded either to the front to cover and protect the photograph in the envelope or to the back to display.

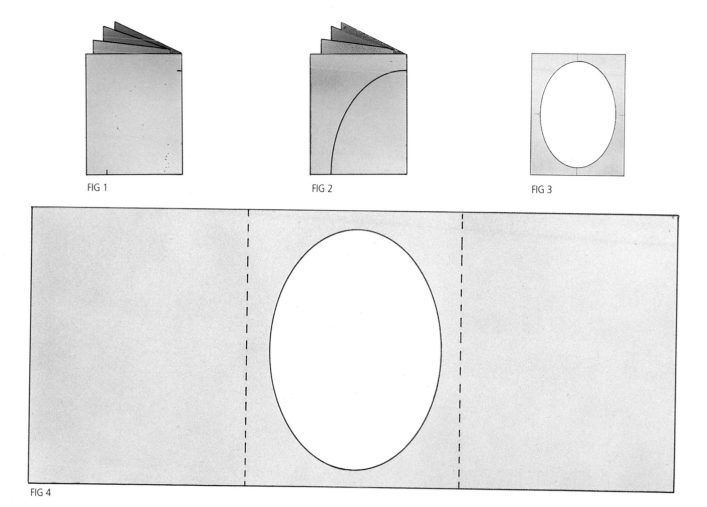

FIG 1

FIG 2

FIG 3

FIG 4

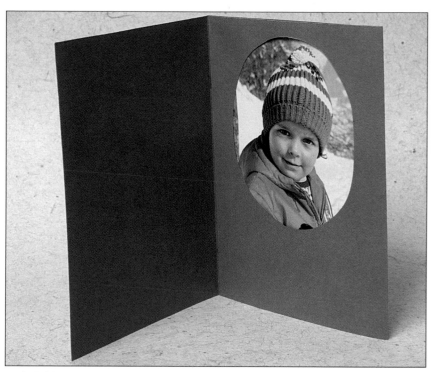

DECORATED FOLDED FRAMES

VARIATION 1

The photograph in this example was framed with a single fold of card. To prevent this delightful picture from being overwhelmed by the strong color of the frame, the card was decorated with sponged-on ink, using shades from the photograph, to soften the color and enhance the picture.

EQUIPMENT

- pencil
- ruler
- craft knife or scalpel
- paper or lightweight card
- small piece of natural sponge
- gouache, acrylic paint or ink

1 Cut a window in one layer of the card and carefully sponge the ink around the border taking care not to color the backing area by protecting it with a sheet of waste paper.

2 Glue the photograph to the uncut area of the card, and then glue the window section on top.

VARIATION 2

A child's drawing was framed in the same manner as the photograph in the previous project, but the size and proportions of this frame are different. There is a wide border, and it is decorated with a stenciled design which complements the picture.

EQUIPMENT

- pencil
- ruler
- craft knife or scalpel
- paper or lightweight card
- stencil material (oil-coated paper, template plastic or acetate)
- stencil brush or sponge
- paint, crayons or felt-tip pens

1 Draw the shapes on the stencil paper and cut out. Try using template plastic or acetate for the stencils so you can see where the design is being positioned.

2 When the stencil is ready, position the cutout shape on the frame and, using paint, crayons or felt-tip pens, apply the color.

3 To hang the completed frame, attach a gummed hook to the back of the card – this type of hook is suitable for lightweight frames only.

ORIGAMI PICTURE FRAME

For this project you will need lightweight paper; you can choose a color that complements your photograph or postcard. If you are planning to frame a standard-sized postcard measuring 5¾in × 4¼in (14.5cm × 10.5cm) with a vertical (or portrait) picture, you will need a piece of paper 11½in × 15½in (29cm × 39cm).

It is easy to adapt the measurements to suit different sizes of pictures. The first measurement should be double the height of the picture and gives the height of the frame. The second measurement will depend on how much, if any, of the paper at the side of the picture you want to show. However, the width of the frame should be at least 2½ times the width of the picture. The picture opening will always be square; it is not necessary to show the whole picture as the width can be adjusted by pushing in the sides. To check whether your measurements are suitable, experiment with a piece of scrap paper.

EQUIPMENT
- pencil
- ruler
- lightweight paper

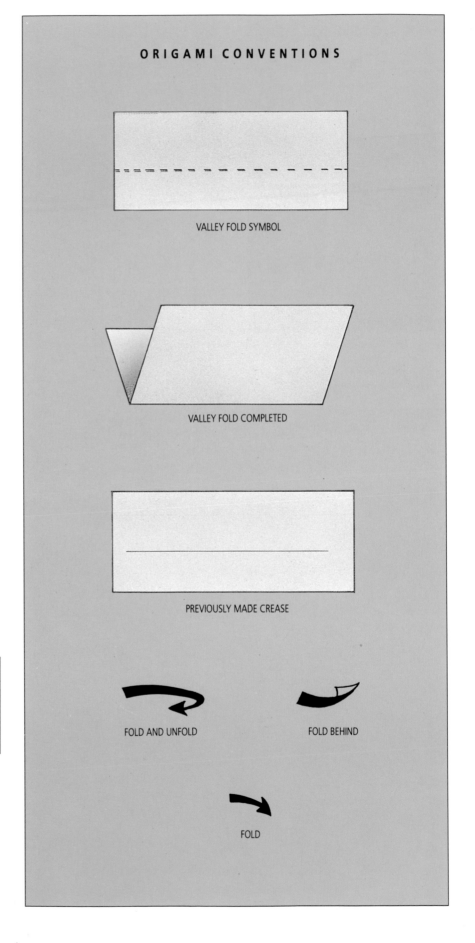

ORIGAMI CONVENTIONS

VALLEY FOLD SYMBOL

VALLEY FOLD COMPLETED

PREVIOUSLY MADE CREASE

FOLD AND UNFOLD

FOLD BEHIND

FOLD

1 Fold the paper in half and then unfold.

2 Fold the two outer edges to the creased center line.

3 Fold the four corners from the center to the outer edge; make sure to fold only the top, single layer of paper.

4 Now, holding the paper with the folds towards you, gently curl the paper away from you so that you tuck the side marked A into the side marked B.

5 The frame is now complete and the picture can be carefully tucked into the diamond-shaped space. For a triangular effect, crease the center back, insert the picture and then crease the two sides. If the postcard to be framed is very stiff, it can be inserted into one side between steps 3 and 4.

T I P S

For readers who are unfamiliar with origami, here are a few helpful tips:

■ Always work on a firm and smooth surface such as a table or large hardback book.

■ Diagrams and instructions are equally important; often one helps to clarify the other. Looking ahead to the next diagram will show how the model should look after the instruction has been carried out.

■ Make the folds slowly and accurately so that the creases are sharp.

FOLDED CORNERS AND BACKING

Another way to display a postcard, photograph or small drawing is to create corners in which to slip the picture. This method is an easy way to make a more decorative presentation than the slit methods explained on page 18.

EQUIPMENT

- lightweight card
- paper
- scrap card
- pencil and ruler
- scissors
- craft knife
- adhesive suitable for card

PREPARATION

To begin, you will need to cut a piece of lightweight card the same size as the picture. This can be colored, but most of it will be hidden by the picture.

You will also need to cut a piece of paper the same size as the picture to be used as a backing. This can be in a color that complements the picture.

1 Using a piece of scrap card, cut a template of one of the shapes in Fig. 1. Now, using the template, cut four shapes from the paper. If the picture is very large or very small, you may have to alter the size of the corner pieces proportionately.

2 On these pieces, score along the dashed lines shown in the diagram.

3 Fold these glue flaps back and position around the piece of card. Glue in place.

4 Now glue the matching piece of paper over the whole of the back so that the glue flaps are covered. It is possible to make an easel as explained on page 48, or to use a frame stand, as shown in the accessories section on page 16.

5 Insert the picture; the frame is finished.

FIG 1

MAT BOARD FRAMES

THOUGHTS ON MATTING **28**

PICTURE COLLAGE **29**

STRAIGHT-CUT MATS **30**

BEVEL-CUT MATS **32**

COVERING MATS WITH PAPER **34**

COVERING MATS WITH FABRIC **36**

MATS WITH EXTRA DEPTH **38**

DOUBLE-WINDOW MATS **40**

DOUBLE MATS **41**

V-CUT AND DOUBLE BEVEL MATS **42**

MATS WITH WASH LINES **44**

MATS WITH PAPER STRIPS **46**

EASELS **48**

SOME THOUGHTS ON MATTING

The use of a mat, even without a frame around it, can and should greatly enhance a piece of artwork. The color and the dimensions of the mat and the material used to make it should all be selected with great care.

A mat should be more than a rim of color surrounding the work. The color should complement the work and link it to the frame if a frame is used. It should also harmonize with the environment in which the finished piece will be displayed.

The width of the mat governs the amount of "space" around the work. This "space" distances the work from its surroundings – for example, "busy" wallpaper. A wide mat also tends to emphasize the work; a narrow one can crowd it.

A mat also protects the work by preventing it from coming into contact with the glass. This contact could cause damage from condensation over a period of time. To further protect the artwork, you should use acid-free materials for the mat even though they may seem expensive. If the piece of work to be framed is valuable, you may want to consider using conservation-quality materials. Until recently mat card was made from untreated wood pulp with high proportions of acid and other impurities which, over a period of time, migrated from the mat into the artwork and caused damage and discoloration. Acid-free matting is made from rag pulp; conservation mat card is made from chemically treated wood pulp. You can also use acid-free backing paper, so that the work is sandwiched between acid-free materials, and acid-free glue and

■ This selection of undecorated mats shows the vast range of color and texture available to the frame maker.

TIPS

Many optical illusions occur with mats:

■ A mat can make the artwork look smaller so it is important to work out the appropriate width for each piece of artwork.

■ Conversely, a mat can give a small picture greater importance.

■ A dark picture surrounded by a light-colored mat will seem smaller than the reverse.

■ The visual center of a picture is always above the geometric center – especially in a "bold" piece of art. If the work is divided exactly in half, the finished appearance will seem top-heavy. To offset this effect, many pictures have a mat that is deeper at the bottom than at the sides and top.

hinges to fix it to the backing material (see page 40). In this way the work is protected as much as possible.

A mat can detract from the art if it is not wisely selected. The mat should complete the piece, not compete with or overwhelm it. Take time over the choice of color and size. Hold corner samples of various colors against the work to check the possibilities. Remember also that matting is available with different textured surfaces, and if a ready-made one is not quite right, you can make your own (see pages 34 and 36). You can also reduce the severity of a mat, if necessary, in several ways, some more simple than others.

These include:
■ added depth (see page 38)
■ double window (see page 40)
■ double mat (see pages 40–41)
■ v-cuts (see page 42)
■ wash-lines (page 44)
■ marbled paper lines (page 46)

PICTURE COLLAGE

An inexpensive and effective way to display a large number of photographs or sketches is to mount them on a large piece of matting, and then hang it or pin it to a bulletin board. The matting can be in a color that makes the pictures stand out if that is the effect you want. This method is an interesting way to display pictures that are not important enough to be framed individually. It might be used as a design source for an artist, for example. The pictures can be fixed to the matting either with glue or with photo-mounts.

STRAIGHT-CUT MATS

The black and white drawing shown in this project was designed on the computer and was so striking that it required a simple, even stark treatment such as this black matting with a black core so that the eye is not drawn to the cut edge. Mats are traditionally cut with a beveled or sloping edge. This leads the eye into the picture, creates an illusion of depth (this can be accentuated by the choice of materials) and prevents shadows from being cast on the work. In this case a straight cut was used so that the shadow it cast would emphasize the perspective of the picture.

It is important to be accurate at all times so the finished work appears professional – inaccuracies show and can cause complications when making the frame.

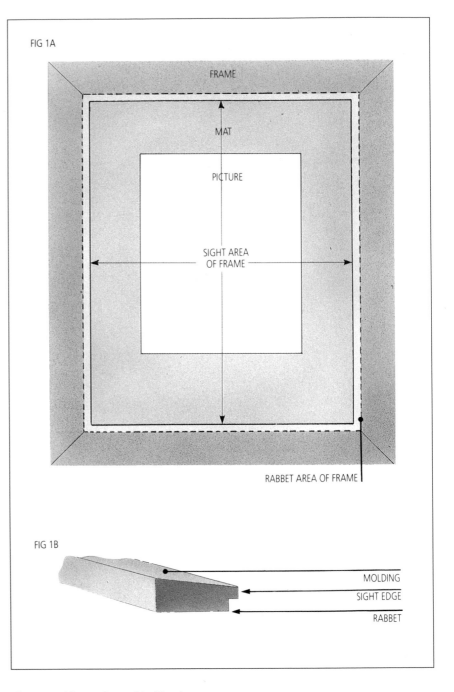

FIG 1A

FRAME

MAT

PICTURE

SIGHT AREA
OF FRAME

RABBET AREA OF FRAME

FIG 1B

MOLDING

SIGHT EDGE

RABBET

EQUIPMENT

- selected matting
- ruler
- pencil
- metal ruler
- triangle
- craft knife
- cutting mat or waste card
- masking, brown paper or fabric tape
- double-sided clear adhesive tape

PREPARATION

■ Start by measuring the area of the artwork that will be visible – in this example 11⅜in × 7¼in (29cm × 18.5cm). This is called the "sight" area. These measurements allow for the mat to cover the edges of the picture by ⅛in (0.3cm).

■ Now decide on the dimensions of the mat: sides and top, 3in (8cm); bottom, 3½in (9cm). With these two sets of measurements you can calculate the overall size of the mat: 17⅜in × 13¾in (44cm × 35cm). If the artwork is to be framed eventually the size of the rabbet of the molding will have some bearing on the overall dimensions of the mat as the rabbet will cover some of it (see Fig. 1a and 1b).

1 Mark the outer edges of the mat carefully on the matting and check to make sure everything is square – right angles at all corners. In this instance a white wax pencil was used so the lines would be clearly visible on the black surface.

3 Now mark the window on the reverse side of the mat. Measure from the outer edges and check to make sure that the corners are square.

5 Now the mat, backing board and picture are ready for assembly. Lay the mat and the backing face down with the top edges touching. Stick them together with masking tape, brown paper tape or fabric tape. This is called hinge matting.

2 Lay the matting on the cutting mat or on waste card. Using a very sharp blade and a metal ruler, cut out the mat and a piece of backing card the same size.

4 The window is now ready to be cut out. Place the mat on the cutting mat or waste card, lay the ruler along the pencil line and, holding the knife at a 90° angle, cut along the line. Hold the ruler very firmly so that it does not move – if necessary clamp it in place.

6 Next, position the picture on the backing board and flip the mat over. By lifting the mat slightly, you can move the picture around until you get it into the right position. Then fix the picture to the backing board with double-sided adhesive tape.

T I P S

■ If the cuts meet in the corners, the window will drop out. If it does not, cut carefully into the corners.

■ A razor blade or emery board can be used to smooth a slightly ragged edge.

■ Keep the piece you cut from the mat for use on a smaller picture or for practice.

■ To fix a valuable piece of artwork to the back board (see step 6), use acid-free paste to attach two small strips of torn acid-free paper to the edge of the picture. Then stick the top of the strips to the backing board with gummed tape.

BEVEL-CUT MATS

For this drawing a single mat with a beveled edge was used (to draw the eye to the drawing). The color was selected to give a "quiet" effect.

EQUIPMENT

- selected matting
- ruler
- pencil
- metal ruler
- triangle
- craft knife
- waste card
- mat cutter

PREPARATION

■ Decide on the "sight" area – this is the amount of the drawing that will be visible through the mat window – 10½in × 12½in (26.5cm × 32cm) in this case. Now decide on the width of the mat – sides and top 2¾in (7.5cm) and bottom 3¼in (8.5cm). With these two sets of measurements, you can calculate the overall size – 16in × 18½in (40.5cm × 47.5cm). Mark this carefully on the sheet of matting and check the measurements to make sure everything is square.

■ Lay the matting on the waste card. Using a very sharp blade, cut out the mat and a piece of backing card the same size.

■ Now mark the window on the reverse side. Measure from the outer edges, and check to see that the corners are square.

1 Position the ruler or straight edge according to the type of mat cutter you use. Make sure the blade is sharp and that it is set to the correct depth for the matting. If the blade is too deep, the cutter will be hard to move and if it is not deep enough, it will not cut through the matting and the window will not drop out.

2 Pay particular attention to the corners – try not to overshoot them as this will show on the right side – they should look like this.

TIPS

■ It is essential to practice on some spare matting to get the feel of the cutter.

■ Do not use a cutting mat with a mat cutter, as bevel-angled cuts do not "self-heal."

■ When cutting the mat, turn it clockwise so you can see the beginning of the previous cut as you approach it and know where to stop.

3 If the cuts are short of the corners, slip the craft knife or a razor blade into the cut, complete the corner and lift out the window.

4 Assemble the mat, backing board and picture as explained in the previous project on page 30.

COVERING MATS: WITH PAPER

In some cases, you may decide that a plain mat would be too severe for the picture you want to frame. One way to deal with this problem is to cover a mat of the appropriate size with some form of decorative paper. Alternatively, the matting itself could be decorated, using either of the techniques already described (see pages 22 and 23).

VARIATION 1

In this example, a shade of blue echoing the delicate blue threads of the Japanese paper contained in the etching was selected for the mat. This element was further emphasized by covering the mat with a semi-transparent Japanese paper with a "lacy" finish which allowed the blue to show through.

EQUIPMENT

- selected matting
- ruler
- pencil
- metal ruler
- triangle
- craft knife
- waste card
- mat cutter
- covering paper
- adhesive suitable for paper
- scrap paper
- roller (optional)

PREPARATION

Cut the mat to size as explained in the previous two projects and cut out the window. It is not essential to cut a beveled edge, but the overall effect will probably be better if you do.

1 Spread glue thinly and evenly over the whole mat – too much glue will soak through the covering paper and not enough will leave an uneven appearance.

2 Position a piece of Japanese paper, cut to the size of the mat plus ¾in (2cm) all around, on the matting and cover with scrap paper. Apply pressure evenly over the four sides and leave to dry under a pile of books.

3 Turn the mat so the Japanese paper is face down, on a clean work surface. Cut diagonally across the outer corners of the paper so that they will be mitered when turned over.

4 Apply glue to the edge of the mat and turn over the edges of the Japanese paper neatly.

5 Cut a window in the center of the paper, leaving a margin of ½in (1.5cm) on all sides. Cut very carefully into the corners so that it is possible to turn over the edges. Apply glue and turn neatly.

6 Finish as described in the previous two projects.

TIPS

- If you plan to frame the matted picture, step 3 could be omited and the paper trimmed to the same size as the mat.
- It is, of course, possible to follow this project using any light- to medium-weight paper. It would be wise to check the reaction of the paper to the glue before starting.

VARIATION 2

The black and white photograph shown here is matted in a striking but simple way. A straight-cut black mat is covered with a medium-weight good quality paper. The outer edges were "deckled" as described below.

EQUIPMENT

- selected matting
- ruler
- pencil
- metal ruler
- triangle
- craft knife
- a sheet of good quality paper
- mat cutter
- fine brush or medicine dropper
- adhesive suitable for paper

1 Using a fine brush or medicine dropper, "draw" a line of water and allow it to soak in for a short time.

2 Then, very gently, pull the edge away from the main area, to create a deckled edge.

3 Glue the paper to the mat and finish as already described.

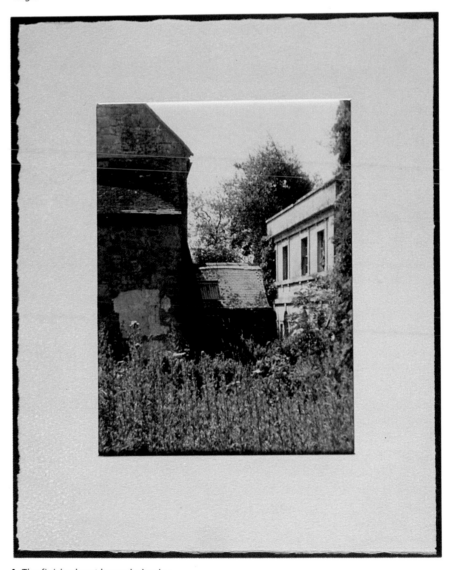

4 The finished mat has a dark edge.

COVERING MATS: WITH FABRIC

This mat is particularly suitable for fabric pictures such as embroidery, tapestry and patchwork because it has a soft look. There is a great feeling of space already contained in the small embroidery chosen for this project and in order to emphasize this, a large and light-colored mat has been used.

EQUIPMENT

- selected matting
- pencil
- metal ruler
- triangle
- craft knife
- waste card
- mat cutter
- covering fabric
- white glue or adhesive suitable for fabric
- scrap paper
- roller (optional)
- iron (optional)

PREPARATION

❚ First, cut the mat to size as explained in earlier projects in this section. Use white or cream matting to make sure the color does not show through the material.

❚ Next cut out the window; it is not essential to cut the mat with a beveled edge, but the overall effect is probably better with a bevel.

❚ Cut a piece of material that is ½in (1.5cm) larger all around than the mat. Try to choose a material that does not fray easily.

1 Apply white glue to the mat in a thin layer and leave to dry. Then position the material on the board, cover with scrap paper and carefully iron over the area – the heat will reactivate the glue. Check that the fabric has no wrinkles and is stuck down all over. Allow to cool under a weight.

2 Turn the mat so that the material is face down on a clean surface. Cut diagonally across the outer corners of the material so that they will be mitered when turned in. Apply glue to the edge of the mat and turn the edges over neatly.

3 Cut a window in the center of the material leaving a margin of ½in (1.5cm) on all sides. Cut very carefully into the corner so that you can turn the edges over. Finish as described previously.

T I P S

❚ Special care should be taken when using velvet to avoid flattening the pile. It may be best to avoid the iron technique for gluing; and if framing the matted print, insert a spacer between the mat and the glass under the molding rabbet (see Fig. 1).

❚ If using ordinary adhesive, disregard step 1 and proceed as follows. Spread glue thinly and evenly over the whole mat – take care as any excess glue will soak through the fabric. Position the material on the mat and cover with scrap paper. Apply pressure evenly over all four sides and leave to dry.

❚ If you want a more padded effect, place a thin foam sheet between the covering fabric and the mat. Foam can also be used to give a padded effect to an embroidered picture before matting; it has the added advantage of absorbing knots and giving a smooth appearance.

4 If the mat is to form part of a conventional frame, omit the previous step and trim the fabric to the same size as the mat.

5 The softness of the fabric-covered mat enhances the work.

FIG 1

MOLDING

GLASS

SPACER

FABRIC-COVERED MAT

ARTWORK

BACKING

HOW TO MAKE A PERFECT OVAL

If you prefer, you can cut an oval window in a mat and cover the area around it with fabric to hide any slight inaccuracies. To draw an oval geometrically, use the following method:

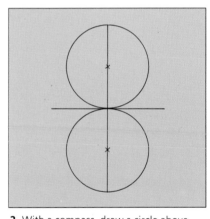

2 With a compass, draw a circle above and below the horizontal (width) line. The radius of each circle will be one-quarter of the vertical (height) line.

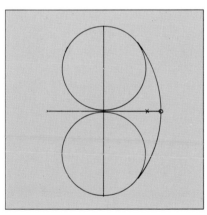

4 With this radius, position the pencil point on one end of the width line, place the compass point on this line and draw an arc joining the two circles on one side.

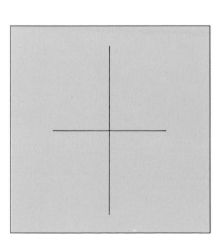

1 Decide on the height of the oval. The width of the oval will be two-thirds of this measurement. Draw these dimensions, in the form of a cross, on the matting.

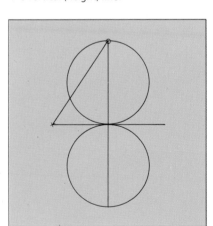

3 Take the compass and position the point at one end of the width line. Extend until the pencil point touches the top of the height line.

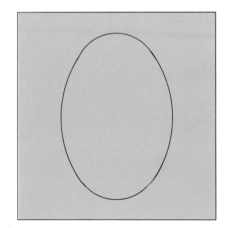

5 Move the pencil point to the other end of the width line and repeat step 4 to complete the oval.

MATS WITH EXTRA DEPTH

On some occasions the artwork to be matted is not completely flat. Although this problem can be solved by making double or triple mats (see page 40) or a box frame (see chapter commencing on page 105), there is another way. Using a material formed by sandwiching polystyrene foam between two lightweight boards, a mat can be cut in the usual way. This material is available in several thicknesses and is extremely lightweight and versatile. It can be covered with paper or fabric as described in the two previous projects; it can also be used to create a space between mats or between mat and artwork (see Figs. 1a and 1b).

E Q U I P M E N T

- foam core board
- metal ruler
- pencil
- triangle
- craft knife
- waste card
- mat cutter
- lightweight covering paper
- glue suitable for paper
- scrap paper

FIG 1A

FOAM BOARD

BACKING BOARD

ARTWORK

MATTING

MATTING

FIG 1B

FOAM BOARD

BACKING BOARD

ARTWORK

MATTING

1 Cut the mat to the required size and prepare as in the project on page 34.

2 Tissue paper is a delicate covering material and two layers should be used for extra strength. To ensure an adequate coverage, glue an extra piece of paper into the window corners.

3 Take particular care when turning in the paper for the window – practice first on a piece of waste to ascertain how far into the corner you should cut.

4 Before gluing, score the paper along the edge of the window so that it turns more easily.

▮ Another simple way to embellish a foam core mat is to make a second mat from a contrasting piece of paper and to place this between the mat and the artwork. A dark "lining" paper will enclose the piece.

5 The finished mat has a three-dimensional look.

DOUBLE-WINDOW MATS

It is sometimes necessary to cut two windows in one mat as for the bond shown here. Other instances where this might be necessary are: topographical or sporting prints which have a title under the print area; a photograph which requires a title that is not part of the design; or a set of small pictures. Take extra care in choosing a color when matting a set of pictures, as the colors in each print may not be identical. The following method has also been used for the multiple mat on page 100.

EQUIPMENT

- selected matting
- metal ruler
- pencil
- tracing paper
- triangle
- craft knife
- waste card
- mat cutter
- acid-free paper
- acid-free paste
- clear adhesive tape

1 The main problem in cutting this style of mat is the accuracy demanded. Plan this project on a piece of tracing paper first with all the measurements written in. It may be helpful to cut a dummy mat from a piece of paper to check the look and dimensions.

2 When you are satisfied with the plan, transfer the measurements to the back of the matting and cut out the windows.

3 This is a valuable piece so it has been fixed to the backing card with acid-free strips of paper and acid-free paste. Tear two strips of paper and paste them to the top edge of the picture.

4 These are then stuck to the backing board with adhesive tape.

5 The strip between the two windows separates the two sections of the bond and adds emphasis to both.

DOUBLE MATS

This type of mat adds interest to a picture and, if it is to be framed, can also create a deeper than normal space between artwork and glass.

The mat closest to the picture is usually a darker color than the outer one. The visible part of the inner mat should be about $\frac{1}{4}$–$\frac{1}{2}$in (0.5–1.5cm wide. If you are using a triple mat, make the visible parts of the inner two mats different widths to avoid a staircase effect. For a purely visual effect, you can use narrow strips of colored paper attached to the reverse of the mat with double-sided adhesive tape (see below).

EQUIPMENT

- selected matting
- pencil
- metal ruler
- triangle
- craft knife
- waste card
- mat cutter
- double-sided clear adhesive tape

An example of a double mat; note that the darker colored material has been used for the inner mat.

Plain or patterned paper can be cut into strips and applied to the back of the mat to create a simple visual effect.

An example of a triple mat. Note the different widths of the two inner mats.

PREPARATION

To cut a double mat accurately, follow this procedure. First decide on size of the window in the inner mat and then decide on the outer dimensions of the finished mat. The dimensions here, for example, are 6½in × 4½in (16.5cm × 11.5cm) for the window and 10in × 8in (25cm × 20cm) for the mat.

First cut the outer mat to size. Then cut the window ¼in (0.5cm) [this width is variable] larger all around than the inner window will be – 7in × 5in (17.5cm × 12.5cm). Do not

remove the window cut-out.

Place strips of double-sided adhesive tape on the back of the mat positioned centrally on all four sides of the window border. Stick another strip of tape in the center of the window cutout which will act as a base for cutting the second window in the inner mat.

1 Cut the inner mat 9½in × 7½in (24cm × 19cm) and place it centrally on the prepared window mat. Mark the window on this, measuring from the edges of the outer mat to ensure accuracy.

2 Working from the back as usual, cut the second window.

3 The two windows can now be removed.

4 Turn over and the double mat is complete.

The subtle appeal of a double mat can be seen here. The shades of the mats and the color of the frame were all chosen to complement the delicate blues and greys of the screenprint.

41

V–CUT AND DOUBLE-BEVEL MATS

Another way to add a creative touch to a picture is to use V-cuts in the mat. There are several variations within this style – matting with a colored core (as used here) can be used to give a stylish effect, or the V-cut can be made wider and used with an inner mat to create a double mat (see Fig. 1a). The same techniques used for the basic V-cut are used to create these additional effects.

EQUIPMENT

- selected matting
- pencil
- metal ruler
- triangle
- craft knife
- waste card
- mat cutter
- double-sided clear adhesive tape
- masking tape

PREPARATION

▌ As always, decide on the size of the window first and mark this on the back of the matting. It may be necessary to make this mat a little larger than usual so that the finished piece has enough "space" to allow for the "break" caused by the V-cut. If unsure, leave the mat excessively large and cut it down after you have completed the bevels.

▌ Decide how far away the V-cut will be from the window edge and mark this second line on the back of the matting. Mark the V-cut line on the right side as well, either very faintly or with a short line near the edge of the mat.

1 First cut the outer window but tape it in place, with masking tape, all around without removing it. Then cut the inner window and tape it in place temporarily.

2 Turn the whole mat to the right side and very carefully cut another bevel along the marked line – the mat cutter should be on the window side of the mat.

▌ Alternatively, cut one mat as usual and then cut a second one with a larger window. From this piece, cut another window larger still and cut a bevel on the right side of this. Place double-sided adhesive tape on both pieces of the outer mat and place carefully in position, applying pressure (see Fig. 1b).

3 The beige–colored mat and the black core revealed in the V-cut harmonize perfectly with the delicately shaded life drawing.

FIG 1A

CROSS-SECTION

FIG 1B

T I P S

There are many different ways of using this type of mat-cutting:

▮ Angles or curves can be cut which will attract attention to areas of the picture (see Fig. 2).

▮ Designs can be cut into the mat to allow a contrasting color, positioned underneath, to show through (see Fig. 3).

▮ A window effect can be created by cutting the mat from three different colors which relate to the picture (see Fig. 4.).

FIG 2

FIG 3

FIG 4

MATS WITH WASH LINES

Lines and washes are traditionally used to decorate the mats of watercolors and prints. They can, however, be used to embellish many other types of picture. It is important that the work be well done because bad workmanship will show. Practice on mat scraps to gain experience and to try out different combinations and spacings. It is also a good idea to test the matting and materials you plan to use to check their compatibility – some inks or felt-tip pens may "bleed" on some matting. Lines can also be used without washes – a good way to unite several small prints or photographs matted together.

The spacing of the lines is important. If they are too far from the window, the eye will not be held; the first line should be no more than ¼in (0.5cm) from the window. A standard and effective pattern of lines and washes is: two lines close together

near the window, then a wide space for the wash line, and finally two or three more lines positioned quite close together. When using the ruling pen, it is a good idea to vary the width of the line by adjusting the space between the points. The widest line will "lead" the eye into the picture and should therefore not be next to the window as the outer lines may seem to disappear.

EQUIPMENT

- selected matting
- metal ruler
- pencil
- plastic ruler
- triangle
- craft knife
- waste card
- mat cutter
- ruling pen
- watercolors
- mixing palette and brushes
- corner marking gauge
- sable (or good quality) brush

T I P S

- If you do not have a corner gauge, try making your own or use a ruler to mark out the line sequence on the mat.
- When selecting the colors for lines and wash, look carefully at the picture and try to choose colors that will harmonize with it.
- When drawing lines, take care not to make the line so wide that the ruling pen runs out of ink – it is impossible to stop and reload the pen without the break showing in the finished piece.
- Your selected wash color should be mixed to a very pale shade and to a thin consistency. If using colored inks, dilute greatly so that the colors do not look too bold – test the color on waste card first.
- When applying a wash, start at one corner and work quickly, so that the first part is still damp when the wash is applied to the last side of the mat. Apply the wash in several thin layers to build up the color if necessary. Have a few cotton swabs nearby as they can be very useful for mopping up excess wash or runs.
- If there are any small imperfections, they can sometimes be removed with a small sharp blade. Or another line might possibly cover the error. It is always worth trying a repair before starting to remake a mat.

1 Take the selected mat and cut the window as usual. Then, using a corner gauge, decide on the sequence (spacing) of the lines and mark them in each corner with a pin or a hard pencil.

2 Load the ruling pen with ink using a brush and wiping it gently against the nib. If dipping the pen directly into the ink, wipe the edges before use.

3 Using a plastic ruler turned upside down to avoid smudging the ink or watercolor – the beveled edge of the ruler will create a space between it and the mat – draw all the lines carefully, working from the inside line outwards and with the outer edge of the mat closest to the body.

■ Felt-tip pens, technical pens or gold marker pens can also be used to create effective lines.

4 Using a brush dipped in clean water, dampen the area between the lines so that the color wash flows evenly onto the mat without leaving any "tide" marks. Then apply the wash using a brush that is close in width to the required wash line.

5 The colors chosen for the lines and wash in the example shown here enhance the rural quality of the watercolor painting. By using a brownish green for the lines and a paler version for the wash, the cream-colored mat becomes almost an extension of the painting.

MATS WITH PAPER STRIPS

Another way of adding decoration to a mat is to use narrow strips of paper or tape. Self-adhesive gold or colored tape, available from specialist shops, can be used in conjunction with lines and washes or on its own. It is also possible to apply this tape to the bevel itself, but this is very tricky. Alternatively, a slim plastic slip fillet, made in several colors, can be placed on either edge of the mat to get this effect.

The spacing of the lines and/or strips is most important. If they start too far from the window, the eye will not be held. Therefore, the first line should be no more than ¼in (0.5cm) from the window. A standard and effective pattern for lines and strips is: two lines close together near the window, then a wider space for a paper or tape strip, and finally more lines positioned quite close together. When using the ruling pen, it is a good idea to vary the width of the lines by adjusting the space between the points.

EQUIPMENT

- selected matting
- pencil
- metal ruler
- triangle
- craft knife
- waste card
- mat cutter
- marbled paper and/or colored tape
- adhesive suitable for paper and/or double-sided clear adhesive tape

PREPARATION

▉ Take the selected mat and cut the window as usual. Decide on the sequence (spacing) of the lines and/or tapes and, using a corner gauge, mark them in each corner with either a pin or a hard pencil.

▉ Mark with a pencil the line that will have the strip – this will act as a guide. Rule the rest of the lines using the chosen medium – ruling pen, felt-tip, marker pen or technical pen.

1 If undertaking much mat decoration of this kind, there is a tool available which can be set to cut several equal strips at a time – a multi-cutter.

2 Cut the strips of paper using a metal ruler to guide the cutter. Take great care in cutting the strips as any inaccuracies will show.

3 Lay the paper or tape strips carefully along the pencil lines. They should overlap at the corners.

4 Using the craft knife, cut through both strips from the window outwards at an angle of 45°. Pull away the excess to leave a cleanly mitered corner. Cover the mat with a clean piece of paper and apply even pressure to the window area to ensure that the strips are completely adhered.

T I P

If self-adhesive paper and tape strips are not available, you can make your own using double-sided clear adhesive tape on decorative paper, but the finished appearance will not be as flat.

5 The strips on the mat pick up the colors in the picture and enhance the overall effect.

■ Here are some variations to a theme: self-adhesive gold tape (right); fine lined paper strip (far right); (and below, from left to right) plastic slip fillet used on the window edge; on the outer edge of the mat; a combined effect with a double mat edged with slim gold plastic slip fillets.

EASELS

There are several ways of making easels for frames – the following diagrams show how to do this. Some are an integral part of the frame, and some are added to the finished frame. The type of easel used often depends on the weight and size of the frame.

EQUIPMENT

- lightweight card or thick card (see directions)
- pencil
- ruler
- craft knife
- glue and/or double-sided clear adhesive tape

CONVENTIONS TO DIAGRAMS

All dotted lines are position guides.
All dashes lines should be scored and creased.
All solid lines should be cut.
All shaded areas require adhesive.

VARIATION 1

The diagram in Fig. 1 shows a very simple support for the type of frame shown on page 18.

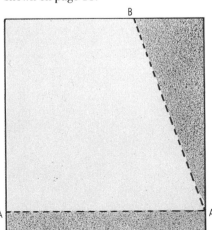

FIG 1

■ Using lightweight card, cut out a piece as in Fig. 1.

■ Score the lines AA and AB as in the diagram.

■ Apply glue or double-sided adhesive tape to the two shaded areas.

■ The base area (AA) is stuck to the center of the stand part of the frame and the upright, triangular area (AB) is stuck to the center of the "frame" back.

■ The angle at which the picture "stands" can be varied by altering the angle of the line AB.

VARIATION 2

The easel or stand shown in Figs. 2 and 3 holds the picture up but is not attached to the frame. The larger the frame, the bigger the stand should be to provide sufficient support.

■ Cut out a strip of lightweight card as shown in Fig. 2 – the area for gluing is slightly narrower than the area to which it will be stuck.

■ Fold into a triangular shape and glue in position as shown in Fig. 3 – make sure to leave a small gap in which to place the picture.

FIG 2

FIG 3

VARIATION 3

The method shown in Fig. 4 is probably the simplest of all, but its use is limited to a few types of frame – the project on page 26, for example.

▌ When making the back of the frame, cut an extra piece of paper or card the same size but preferably in a lighter-weight material than used for the front of the frame.

▌ Cover the back of the frame as instructed in the project and then score the easel piece and glue the shaded area directly on top of the frame back.

FIG 4

VARIATION 4

The two easels shown in Figs. 5 and 6 and Figs. 7 and 8 are similar and both are made of thicker card than the previous ones. The main difference between them is that the easel in Figs. 5 and 6 is fixed to the frame back. The easel in Figs. 7 and 8 is fixed to the support and slides under the upper tab – this is easier to make. These easels and frame backs should be made before the two halves of the frame are put together. The frames look better if the inside of the back is lined with a piece of harmonizing paper; then, when the picture is removed, the hole left by the support does not show from the front.

FIG 7

FIG 8

FIG 5

FIG 6

CLAY AND PAPIER-MACHE

PAPIER-MACHE MIRROR FRAME **52**

PAPIER-MACHE PICTURE FRAME **56**

CLAY FRAME **58**

PAPIER-MACHE MIRROR FRAME

Papier-mâché frames are fun to make for both children and adults. As they are made from paper, they are extremely light in weight, but they can be made to look very ornate with a little experience. It is easy to get carried away when decorating these frames, so take care not to overpower the contents of the frame.

The two examples shown in this section are very different. The basic method – described below – has been used to frame a mirror, and the decoration is quite striking. The picture frame described in the second project on page 56 has less decoration as the shape is part of the design and the picture in the frame is powerful. The background color has been chosen to harmonize with the picture.

Papier-mâché can be decorated in a number of ways – painting or drawing directly onto the shape, using stencils or with collage. Both of the examples in this chapter have been decorated using paint. The shape in the basic example following has only the edge painted as the center will be covered by the mirror.

PREPARATION

▌ Cover the working area with an old cloth or newspapers and prepare the adhesive – either mix up the wallpaper paste according to the directions on the package or dilute the white glue with three parts glue to one part water.

▌ Take the mold and cover the inside with vaseline or cling wrap so that the papier mâché will be easy to remove when the layers are completed.

1 Tear strips of newspaper, dampen them and lay them neatly across the mold. Try to keep the strips as flat as possible by tearing them to fit.

2 When the mold is covered, paint the surface liberally with the paste or thinned white glue.

3 Now add the next layer. It is a good idea to use a colored tissue paper, so that layers can be seen clearly and the paper built up evenly on the mold.

4 When the mold is covered, brush on more paste or glue. Continue to build up the layers in this way until there are about eight layers. Put the mold in a warm place and leave it for about 24 hours to dry.

E Q U I P M E N T
- old newspapers
- colored tissue paper
- wallpaper paste or thinned white glue
- polystyrene plate as a mold
- vaseline or cling wrap
- scissors
- sandpaper
- paint brushes
- water-based paint for undercoat
- paint and varnish
- circular mirror
- quick-setting adhesive

5 Carefully remove the paper from the mold and trim the edges.

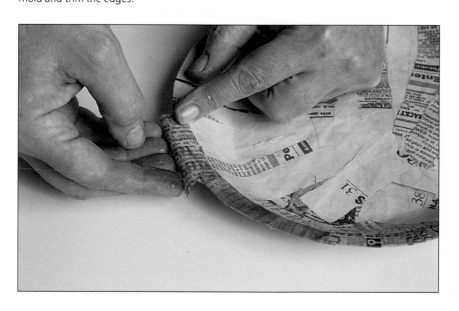

6 To get an even edge, bind the cut edge with two layers of paper. When the edges are dry, sand away any unevenness with a medium to fine grade sandpaper and then paint the shape on both sides with two layers of undercoat. This will ensure an even base for the final decoration.

7 Draw around the mirror and then sketch in the design on the frame with a pencil.

8 Mix the paints — gouache or poster paint — to an appropriate consistency and paint in the design.

9 The black paint adds the final touch to the design as well as covering slight mistakes. The reverse side can either be painted with a single color or decorated. For durability, give the finished frame three coats of varnish.

10 On the back of the mirror, put a generous amount of adhesive in the center and ½in (1.5cm) all around the edge. Then, placing the mirror in the correct position on the frame, press down firmly and hold until the adhesive has set. If the frame is slightly uneven, this pressure will take care of the problem.

11 Use the same strong adhesive to fix a hanger to the back of the mirror frame, and suspend it from a hook.

PAPIER-MACHE PICTURE FRAME

EQUIPMENT

- old newspapers
- colored tissue paper
- wallpaper paste or thinned white glue
- pre-sealed cork floor tiles
- craft knife
- scrap card or construction paper for template
- masking tape
- sandpaper
- paint brushes
- water-based paint for undercoat
- paint and varnish
- thin wooden batten
- quick-setting adhesive
- backing board
- turn clips or tacks

PREPARATION

First, decide on the size and shape of the frame, and then make a template from the scrap card or construction paper. The template can be a half or quarter of the frame if the frame is symmetrical.

TIP

If the picture is to be permanently fixed into the frame, the measurement for the backing board should be taken from the outer edges of the wooden battens. Place the picture into the frame and, using tacks, secure the backing board in place.

1 Draw around the template on the tiles to form the shape of the frame.

2 Cut out the shape with a craft knife.

3 Unless the frame is quite small, the tiles may not be large enough. In this case the tiles were joined with masking tape wrapped around the cut shape.

4 Using the method already described on pages 52 and 53, cover the back and front of the "frame" with layers of newspaper and colored tissue paper. It is not necessary to use vaseline or cling wrap as the cork becomes part of the frame and there is no mold to remove. When sufficient layers have been applied, leave the frame to dry. Turn it over from time to time so that both sides dry evenly.

5 When the frame is dry, sand away any unevenness with a medium to fine grade sandpaper and then paint it on both sides with two layers of undercoat. This will ensure an even base for the final decoration.

6 Sketch the design around the frame with a pencil. Mix the paints — gouache or poster paint — and paint in the design. Remember to paint the reverse side of the frame to harmonize with the basic color.

7 The black paint adds definition to the shape as well as covering slight mistakes. For durability, the finished frame has been given three coats of varnish.

8 On the back of the frame, mark the size of the picture — this will give the line for the inside edge of the battens. Cut two lengths of batten for the sides and two lengths for the top and the bottom. Spread the quick setting adhesive along the battens and fix to the marked positions on the back of the frame, holding firmly.

9 If the picture is to be interchangeable, the backing board should be the same size as the picture. Attach the turn clips to the battens — the number used will depend on the size of the frame. Place the picture and the backing board in the frame and lock into position by turning the clips.

10 This highly decorated papier-mâché frame would make an interesting decoration even without an insert.

▨ The same template was used to make the frame shown here, but was simply painted in one color and then varnished.

▨ A simple stenciled design can produce an equally pleasing effect.

CLAY FRAME

A small decorative frame can be made using clay. A kiln is not a necessity as you can use self-hardening clay or substitute products, available from craft shops, for this project. If you use self-hardening clay, find out about the special glazes for it. Clay or clay substitutes should be used only for small frames – a maximum size of 6in (15cm) in diameter or 5in (12.5cm) square – because a larger frame could warp.

E Q U I P M E N T

- clay of selected type
- rolling pin
- piece of rigid plastic on which to roll out clay
- ruler
- pencil
- craft knife
- template
- 2 pieces of scrap hardboard a little larger than proposed frame size
- fine sandpaper
- card for backing
- paper adhesive for picture
- impact adhesive for finishing
- paint
- varnish
- brushes

P R E P A R A T I O N

Decide on the size of the frame. A rectangular frame is easiest to make because you can use strips of clay. For a circular frame, you have to use a round template about 1in (2.5cm) thick.

1 Working on the piece of rigid plastic to keep the clay from sticking to the work surface, knead and flatten the clay. Then roll it out until it is about ¼in (0.5cm) thick and as long as the proposed frame.

2 Using the ruler so the edges will be completely straight, cut four strips about 1in (2.5cm) wide.

3 On one piece of scrap hardboard, draw pencil lines for guidance. Then place the strips of clay in position; the two side strips first, then the two remaining strips across the top and bottom. These strips will overlap the side strips.

4 Now miter the corners by cutting diagonally through both strips from the inside of the frame to the outside. Remove the waste pieces.

5 Next moisten the cut edges at each corner and score with the knife point so that the surfaces are slightly rough; then press them together.

6 Smooth the top surface with the knife; if necessary, dampen slightly. This step is most important.

TIPS

The frame can be decorated in different ways:

▮ It can be simply painted as in this project, or additional shaped pieces of clay can be added to it. These pieces should be cut from the remains of the clay rolled out for the frame. Roll it out a little thinner and stick the shapes to the frame with moistened clay. If necessary, the design can be attached with a suitable glue.

▮ Whichever method of decoration you choose, varnish the frame when it is finished.

▮ Cut a piece of the backing card the same size as the frame and fix the picture in the center of the card. The picture should be slightly larger than the window of the frame. If you wish to change the picture frequently, attach it with photo-corners.

▮ To finish the frame, fix the backing card to the frame with glue or, if the picture is to be interchangeable, with narrow strips of self-adhesive Velcro on the frame and the backing.

▮ To display the frame, attach an easel to the backing (see pages 48–50) to make it free-standing or fix a gummed hanger very securely to the back.

7 Place the second piece of scrap hardboard on top of the frame and carefully turn the "sandwich" over. Lift off the hardboard and check to see that the joins are smooth on this side. Replace the hardboard, place a book on top to prevent the frame warping and/or cracking and leave to dry. When the frame is dry, gently smooth away any rough edges with sandpaper.

8 Using poster paints or gouache, paint the base color onto the frame and allow to dry.

9 The frame can be further decorated, and varnished with a product compatible with the clay used.

CUT-OUT FRAMES

BASIC METHOD **62**

STAIN FINISH **66**

DECOUPAGE FINISH **67**

SHAPED WINDOW **68**

SHAPED OUTLINE **69**

BASIC METHOD

This frame is relatively quick to make and allows for simple or elaborate decoration. As it is made from a flat piece of wood, there is no need for special equipment or for great accuracy. This type of frame is not suitable for valuable pieces of work, however, because the picture is not sealed into the frame and is vulnerable to the atmosphere.

EQUIPMENT

- pencil
- ruler
- craft knife or scalpel
- lightweight card
- birch plywood (¼in or 0.5cm thick)
- thin hardboard
- batten strips (⅛in or 0.3cm thick)
- hand drill
- small saw
- fret saw
- keyhole board
- clamps
- sandpaper and wood adhesive
- paint
- brushes
- varnish

PREPARATION

■ As with previous projects, decide on the window and the overall size of the frame first. Draw the overall measurements on the piece of wood and cut the piece to size or have this done at the suppliers. Birch plywood is the easiest type with which to work – it cuts smoothly and can be finished to a high standard. Other types of plywood do not have these advantages.

■ Next, prepare the wood – a little extra effort at this stage will save time later. Working in the direction of the grain (visible on the surface of the wood), gently sand the top surface. Take a damp cloth and wipe over the surface so that the area looks damp but is not saturated. Allow to dry completely. The surface will now feel slightly "hairy" – this is called "raising the grain" and occurs only once. If this were to happen when the frame was being painted, it would not be possible to sand the surface without spoiling the paintwork. Now sand the surface again – the wood should feel satin-smooth.

■ Next, draw the "window" on the piece of wood. Drill a small hole in a corner of the window area of the wood so that the blade of the fret saw can be inserted. If the window is square or rectangular, it might be easier to make a hole in each corner to avoid having to negotiate the corners with the fretsaw. Sometimes you have to drill more than one hole because the "throat" of the fret saw will not reach part of the line and you have to work from two directions to cut it.

■ Some of the more unusual pieces of equipment needed for the following projects: a keyhole board, fret saw and G-clamps.

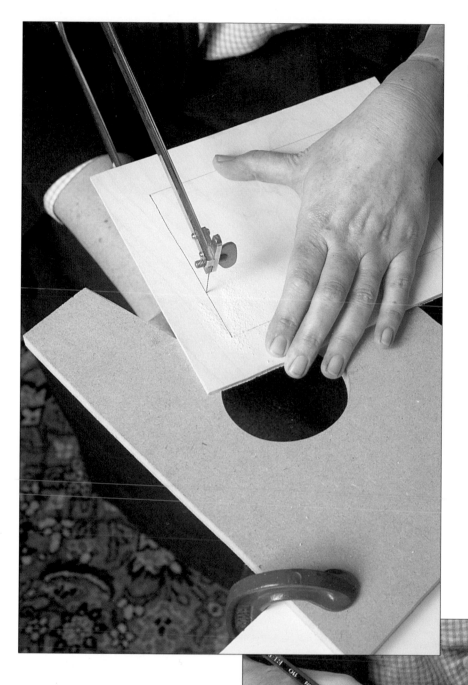

1 Tighten the blade in the frame. Supporting the piece of wood on the keyhole board, cut slowly and evenly along the marked line. With the sandpaper, smooth away any unevenness along the cut edge and clean up the corners if necessary.

2 The next step is to decorate the frame. Turn it to the right side and lightly draw the design on the wood. This design has been drawn on paper and transferred using carbon paper.

63

4 Cut a piece of hardboard the same size as the frame to be used as backing, and then cut batten strips to fit the back of this board. You will need three batten strips – two side strips and a bottom strip; the picture will be inserted from the top. Glue the strips to the edges of the backing. Measure between the inner edges of the strips and cut a piece of lightweight card to fit. The picture will be attached to this.

3 Using good quality brushes and paints diluted to a suitable consistency, paint the design on the frame. You may want to practice the technique on the window cut-out first – painting on wood is not difficult, but the surface feels very different from paper.

5 The frame front can now be glued together – if the frame is large, you may want to tap in a few small tacks from the back.

6 Finally, varnish the whole frame. Build up at least three layers before sanding very lightly with the finest grade of sandpaper. Then add a final coat of varnish.

7 Attach the picture in the correct position to the lightweight card and slide into the completed frame. This frame can be hung or it can be free-standing. To hang, attach screw eyes and picture wire. A sheet of acetate, cut to size, could be inserted in front of the picture to provide a little protection.

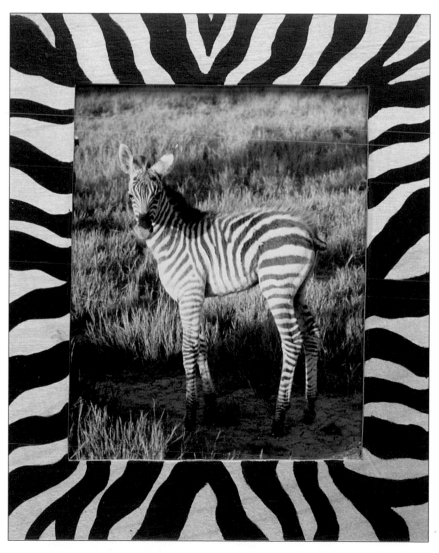

8 The wood of the frame and the zebra stripes decorating it emphasize the wildlife setting of the picture.

STAIN FINISH

This frame is made exactly the same way as the one in the previous project; only the style of finish is different. Since the sepia tone of the picture seemed to require a straightforward and unfussy finish, a natural colored wood stain was used. Other choices for this frame might have been a wood stain in non-wood colors (see page 68) or a thinned wash of paint (see page 70).

EQUIPMENT

- as for previous project
- wood stain

PREPARATION

Complete the frame as for the preceding project up to the decorating stage.

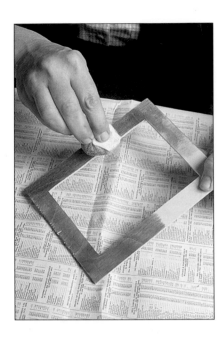

1 With a clean, soft rag soaked with stain, wipe the surface of the frame. Try to work evenly and quickly so that there will be no "tide marks" to show the beginning and end of each stroke. Build up the color with several layers of thinned stain. When you have achieved the right depth of color, apply varnish to seal the surface.

2 Finish the frame, following steps 4, 5 and 7 in the previous project.

DECOUPAGE FINISH

Follow the same procedure for making this frame as for making the one on page 62; the directions below are for the finish. To retain the natural quality suggested by the sepia tone of the picture, the natural color of the birch plywood was maintained. It was embellished with paper cutouts in keeping with the subject of the picture.

EQUIPMENT

- as for project on page 62
- scissors
- tweezers (optional)
- white glue
- paper patterns

PREPARATION

■ Complete the frame up to the decorating stage. Then, decide on the shape of the cutouts and prepare them. Make sure that their size is appropriate for the width of the frame.

■ Place the cutout pieces in position on the frame and move around until you are satisfied with the overall appearance. You may wish to mark these positions lightly on the wood.

1 Brush the wrong side of the cutout pieces with glue. Use the glue sparingly so it will not ooze out at the sides. Removing excess glue without disturbing the other pieces can be difficult.

2 Place one piece in the correct position on the frame using the tweezers if you wish. With a clean, soft cloth, press firmly on the piece being careful not to move it.

3 Fix all the pieces in this way and allow the glue to dry completely.

4 Build up and protect the surface of the frame with at least six coats of varnish. Allow each coat to dry thoroughly before applying the next.

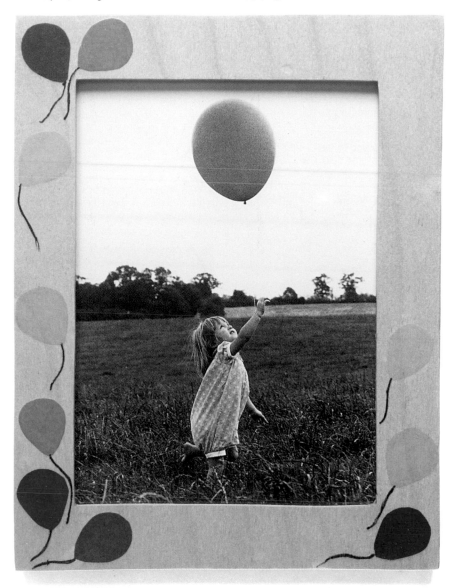

SHAPED WINDOW

The window of this frame is shaped to provide added interest. This type of frame is best used for a picture that is very special and one that will remain in the frame for some time. It could also be used as a gift, but in this case choose a fairly simple shape for the window – a curve or a zig-zag, for example, depending on the effect you want to achieve.

1 First decide on the outer dimensions of the frame and the overall size of the window. Place a piece of tracing paper over the picture; work out the shape of the window and draw it on the tracing paper. Take care not to press so hard with the pencil that the picture is marked.

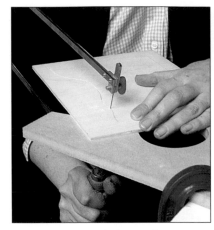

3 Drill holes through the wood, cut out and complete the frame as in the previous projects, using whichever finish seems most suitable.

EQUIPMENT

- soft pencil
- ruler
- craft knife or scalpel
- construction paper
- tracing paper
- lightweight card
- masking tape
- birch plywood (¼in or 0.5cm thick)
- hardboard
- batten strips – as thin as possible
- hand drill
- small saw
- fret saw
- keyhole board
- clamps
- sandpaper
- wood adhesive
- paint
- brushes
- varnish

2 When the design is ready, transfer the window shape to a piece of construction paper and cut out. Place the template on the prepared wood and draw around it.

TIP

The pattern could also be transferred to the wood by drawing over the lines on the reverse side of the tracing paper. Then, with the right side up, place the tracing paper in exactly the right position on the piece of wood and stick down with the tape. Now go over the design and it will be transferred to the surface of the wood.

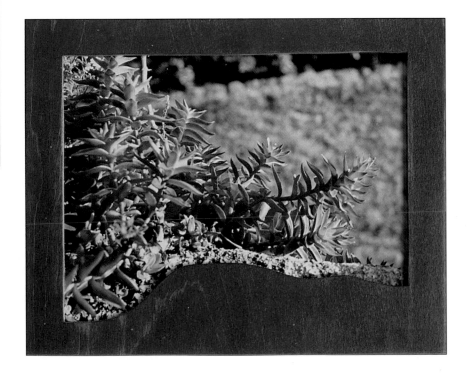

4 The effect here was achieved using colored wood stain and varnish.

SHAPED OUTLINE

Both the outline and the window of this frame have been shaped to provide added interest. In this type of frame, the shapes should be chosen to complement, or at least not fight, each other. As a general rule, the window can only be rectangular if the frame has an extended shape (see Figs. 1 and 2). If the outer shape is cut away, the rectangular window looks wrong (see Fig. 3).

EQUIPMENT

- soft pencil
- ruler
- craft knife or scalpel
- construction paper
- lightweight card
- masking tape
- birch plywood (¼in or 0.5cm thick)
- hardboard
- batten strips – as thin as possible
- hand drill
- small saw
- fret saw
- keyhole board
- clamps
- sandpaper
- wood adhesive
- paint
- brushes
- varnish

FIG 1

FIG 2

FIG 3

1 Having decided on the overall dimensions of the frame and the size of the window, place a piece of tracing paper over the picture. Draw the dimensions on the tracing paper and work out the chosen shape within these measurements.

2 When the design is ready, draw the outline and window shapes on the piece of paper and cut out a template. Position the template on the prepared piece of wood and draw around the outer outline. Remove the template and cut out the shape. Reposition the template on the shaped piece of wood and draw around the window. Remove the template.

3 Drill holes, insert the blade and cut out the window as for previous projects. When this has been done, complete the frame as before using whichever finish seems most suitable.

4 For a simple paint wash effect, mix the chosen color and dilute until the desired intensity is acquired. Test on a piece of scrap plywood.

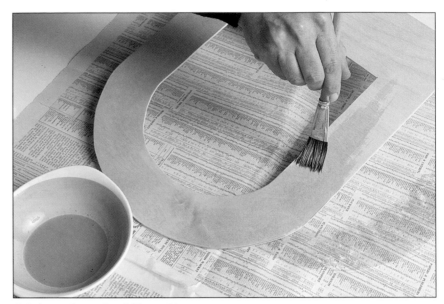

5 Paint on the wash quickly, stroking on the color in the direction of the grain.

6 The shape chosen for this frame was determined by the picture itself. The curve echoes the arch of the gateway and is a simple shape to draw and cut.

WOODEN FRAMES

BUTTED EDGES **72**

MITERED JOINTS **74**

MITERED FRAME WITH SLIP LINER **82**

BUTTED EDGES

The easiest wooden frame to make is one with butt joints. As this looks quite chunky, it is ideal for heavy or thick items such as tiles. The tiles are glued to a base and four strips of wood are nailed to the base around them. Here, compartments have been created for each tile.

This type of frame would also be useful for a piece of tapestry or a painting that is already on a stretcher and does not require glass. Simply cut two strips of wood the height of the painting and nail them to the sides of

FIG 1

the stretcher. Then cut another two strips the width of the painting plus the side strips and nail them in position, using two nails in each corner (see Fig. 1). The wood strips can be stained or painted and varnished before they are nailed in place.

EQUIPMENT

- tiles
- strips of wood
- wood for base (plywood or similar)
- ruler
- pencil
- tenon saw
- adhesive suitable for wood
- brads
- adhesive suitable for tiles (optional)

PREPARATION

Decide on the arrangement of the tiles and then work out the dimensions of the frame. These tiles are arranged in a square; add the width of the strips of wood to the measurement of the tiles to get the finished size of the base.

1 Lay the tiles on an oversize piece of wood or hardboard. Measure and cut two side strips of wood and the vertical central divider. Place these three strips in position and measure the length of the two remaining outer strips.

2 Cut these and place around the tiles.

3 With the tiles in position, measure and cut the two horizontal dividers.

4 Now you can measure accurately the size of the base. Cut the base and glue the strips of wood to the outer edges.

5 Working from the back, mark the position for the brads to secure the outer strips – a distance of half the width of the strip in from the edge.

6 Hammer in the brads. Still working from the underside, mark the position of the dividers – in this case they will be placed centrally. Drill the holes and turn the frame over.

7 Lay the tiles in position and check that the holes are under the dividers. Then glue the dividers in place, remove the tiles and nail from underneath.

8 The frame is now ready for the tiles. These can either be glued in position using tile adhesive or they can be held in place by small tacks tapped into the frame and dividers.

9 Varnish or paint the frame as desired. Screw in the hangers.

MITERED JOINTS

This is the most traditional type of frame and in some ways the most difficult to make well. A certain amount of specialized equipment is necessary; this is listed below at the beginning of the project. Some of the tools are general household tools; the specialized framing tools are moderately priced and easily found. For a professional framer, more mechanized equipment is available.

The miter joint used in picture framing is the weakest type of joint, as compared to dovetail or mortise joints, because it is end to end and for this reason accuracy is essential. There are ways of making this type of frame other than the one used here, but the following method is the simplest way to achieve an adequate result with a minimum of equipment.

EQUIPMENT

- sharp pencil
- ruler
- molding
- miter box or corner clamp
- saw
- frame clamp
- adhesive suitable for wood
- glass
- glass cutter
- T-square
- brads
- power or hand drill
- tack hammer
- nail set
- wood filler
- stain
- hardboard
- Stanley knife or similar
- brown gummed tape or masking tape

PREPARATION

■ The first step in making the frame is to work out accurately the size of the frame and, from this, to calculate the amount of molding needed. Measure the piece to be framed – this may or may not include a mat. This size will be the measurements of the frame between the rabbets (see Fig. 1) plus an allowance of about ⅛in (0.3cm) for ease.

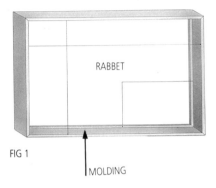

RABBET

FIG 1

MOLDING

■ To calculate how much molding is needed for a frame, use this formula: add the all around measurement of the artwork plus eight times the width of the molding plus a small allowance for cutting (see Figs. 2a and 2b).

■ For the matted certificate framed here, the amount of molding required was calculated as follows: the mat measures 15¾in × 11¾in and the molding is ¾in wide; 2 × (15¾in × 11¾in) = 55 + (8 × ¾) = 61in plus a cutting allowance of 2in adds up to 63in of molding needed.

■ Alternatively, using metric measurements, the mat measures 40cm × 30cm and the molding is 2cm wide; 2 × (40 + 30) = 140 + (8 × 2) = 156cm plus cutting allowance of 4cm = 160cm; 160cm of molding was needed.

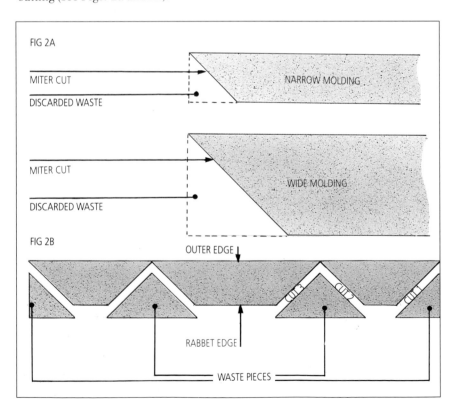

FIG 2A

MITER CUT

DISCARDED WASTE

NARROW MOLDING

MITER CUT

DISCARDED WASTE

WIDE MOLDING

FIG 2B

OUTER EDGE

CUT 3   CUT 2   CUT 1

RABBET EDGE

WASTE PIECES

■ If possible, make sure that the miter box or clamp is fixed to the work surface.

■ If the miter box is new, use the saw to mark the cross cut on the base so there is a line with which to align the pencil mark.

■ If you are using a new miter clamp and saw, put a little grease on the surface of the blade to make it run smoothly.

■ Be sure to check that the base of the molding is flat in the box or clamp before cutting, otherwise the cut will not be vertical and the joins will not fit.

■ If using a clamp, make sure that the pressure of the clamp does not mark the molding – protect very soft molding with a piece of card.

■ When cutting a very large frame, it may be necessary to support the molding that extends beyond the box or clamp on some blocks of wood.

■ When cutting, use the saw smoothly and with light pressure – if you are heavy-handed, the saw will "jump" and you may get a poor cut.

■ Before gluing the frame together, note that some woods are more absorbent than others and this will affect the amount of glue required and the length of drying time. If possible, check out the glue on some leftover molding.

■ If the frame is quite deep, pin it together (see step 8) while the frame clamp is still in position so there will be no chance of the join coming undone.

MAKING THE FRAME

■ Prepare to cut one of the long sides of the frame. First, using the corner clamp, cut a miter at the end of the length of molding to give a clean edge (see Fig. 2b – cut 1).

1 Now measure and mark the length of the first long side on the inside of the rabbet.

2 Line up the pencil mark on the molding with the cross-cut in the miter box or clamp, allowing for the saw cut – a few practice cuts will show how much to allow. Make the second cut – (see Fig. 2b – cut 2) – note the angle of this cut is opposite to the angle of the first.

3 Next, cut off the waste piece (see Fig. 2b – cut 3).

5 Before assembling the frame, rub the cut edges against the rough side of the hardboard to smooth them and then trim off any "whiskers" with a razor blade or craft knife. Do not use sandpaper as this would rub away too much and affect the fit of the join.

4 Measure the second long side, against the piece which has just been cut. On a firm surface, hold the two pieces of molding back to back and mark the exact length of the first piece on the outside of the molding; check the measurement with a ruler. Place the molding in the miter box or clamp as above and check as before. Then cut the second piece and lay both pieces aside. Repeat the above procedures to cut the two short pieces for the frame. There are now four pieces.

6 Working on a flat surface, lay the pieces close together in the correct positions and place the frame clamp around the outside with the pulling piece on the right-hand side (assuming the framemaker is right-handed). Remove the short pieces and apply glue.

7 Replace the short pieces in their correct positions and tighten the frame clamp by pulling up the cord. When it is really tight, secure it firmly – the cord should "ping" when pulled. Wipe off any excess glue and set the frame aside to dry for a few hours. Remove the frame clamp and check that there is no excess glue in the rabbet. If there is, remove it with a craft knife or razor blade.

8 The frame is now ready to be pinned. The brads will go in more easily if you drill small holes through the molding for them. Cut off the head of a brad and insert the shaft into the drill as a bit. This ensures that the holes are the right size. If the molding is narrow, one brad per corner is enough. The brads should be placed in the sides of the frame for strength, but they do show a little. For aesthetic reasons, brads are sometimes placed in the top and bottom pieces.

9 Hammer in the brads using the nail set to drive them below the surface of the wood. Fill the holes with filler and stain to match.

CUTTING THE GLASS

The next stage is to cut the glass. Unless the frame is very large, this is not too difficult. Use a good glass cutter – the more expensive the tool, the better it will be – and take good care of it. Keep the cutting head standing on a rag soaked in household oil diluted with paint thinner.

Picture glass is thinner than window glass and quite fragile to handle in sheet form. Try a few practice cuts first. Most people hold the glass cutter between the index and middle finger for good control but this is not essential. Be sure to hold the cutter at a constant angle.

Once you master the glass cutting technique, you are ready to cut the glass to size. The glass should be cut the same size as the piece of work being framed. When measuring the glass, allow for the cutter's width against the ruler – about ⅛in (0.3cm).

1 Lay the glass so that it overhangs the work surface slightly and position the T-square along its edge. Hold the glass cutter fairly upright and keep the arm extended so that the body moves back rather than the elbow bending.

2 Draw the cutter along the surface of the glass with an even pressure – there should be an audible "hiss". Break the glass (see below) and repeat the process for the other dimension.

BREAKING THE GLASS

There are several ways to break the glass after scoring it:

1 Hold the glass in both hands on both sides of the line and press up with the fingers and down with the thumbs.

2 Place the glass on the edge of the work surface with the score line parallel to the edge and press down gently.

3 Lift the glass and place a pencil under the score line. Press down on both sides.

4 Lift the glass and, from underneath, tap along the score line with the end of the cutter.

FINISHING THE FRAME

▌ The hardboard for the backing can be cut to size in almost the same way you cut the glass using a Stanley knife. Draw the knife along the straight edge several times and then break by applying hand pressure.

▌ Fix D-rings to the hardboard or screw rings in the molding for hanging. If you use D-rings, insert them at this stage. They should be positioned one-third of the way down from the top and 2–3in (5–8cm) in from the sides depending on the size of the frame.

1 Mark the correct position and pierce with a bradawl. Place the D-ring in position and insert the rivet through the hole. Turn over the hardboard and, working on a hard surface, split the rivet and hammer it flat.

2 All the components of the frame are now ready to assemble. Place the glass in the frame from the back and clean the inside. Next put in the piece of work for which the frame has been made.

3 Put in the hardboard and secure it with a few brads or glazier's points. If you plan to do much framing, you can get a special tool called a point driver.

4 Take the tape and stick it to the back of the frame to protect the contents of the frame from the atmosphere.

5 Trim the overlap at the corners for a neat appearance. If using screw rings, insert them and the wire or cord; the picture is complete.

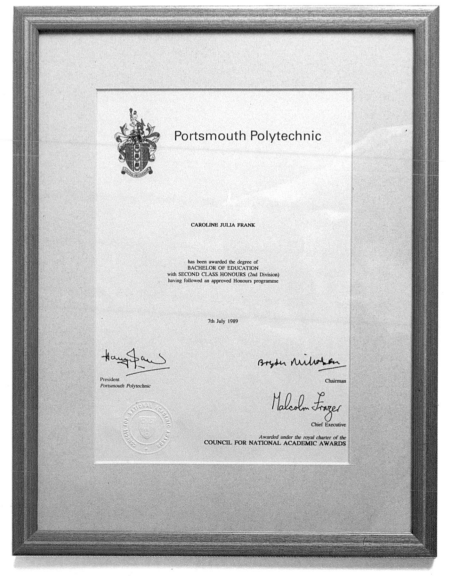

Portsmouth Polytechnic

CAROLINE JULIA FRANK

has been awarded the degree of
BACHELOR OF EDUCATION
with SECOND CLASS HONOURS (2nd Division)
having followed an approved Honours programme

7th July 1989

President
Portsmouth Polytechnic

Chairman

Chief Executive

Awarded under the royal charter of the
COUNCIL FOR NATIONAL ACADEMIC AWARDS

6 With a little practice, truly professional results can be achieved.

MITERED FRAME WITH SLIP LINER

Slip liners or inserts are often used for pictures or articles that require distancing from the frame. They are also used frequently with oil or acrylic paintings and other works that do not require glass. They can be used to create box frames with glass as shown on page 106. Best described as frames within frames, they provide a soft transition from the artwork to the frame and surroundings.

The method for framing this picture is much the same as that used for the basic mitered frame on page 74. The main difference is that the slip liner fits into the outer frame snugly – if it stays in place without any glue or brads then the framer has done an excellent job. However, it is quite permissible to secure the slip frame in place with brads if necessary.

EQUIPMENT

- sharp pencil
- ruler
- molding
- slip liner
- miter box or corner clamp
- saw
- frame clamp
- adhesive suitable for wood
- brads
- power or hand drill
- tack hammer
- nail set
- wood filler
- stain

COVERING A MITERED FRAME

Slip liners are often covered with fabric – the one used in this example was purchased as shown. However, if a suitable one cannot be found, you can make your own quite easily using a simple flat or rounded molding (see Figs. 1–3).

■ First make up a mitered frame as described in the previous project. Then cover this frame with strips of fabric (see Fig. 1).

■ Letting the fabric overhang both edges of the molding, glue in place. Miter the corners and peel away waste areas A and B (see Fig. 2).

■ Then glue the fabric neatly into place along the "sight" edge of the molding. Trim the other edge flush with the molding – this will be under the rabbet of the outer frame (see Fig. 3).

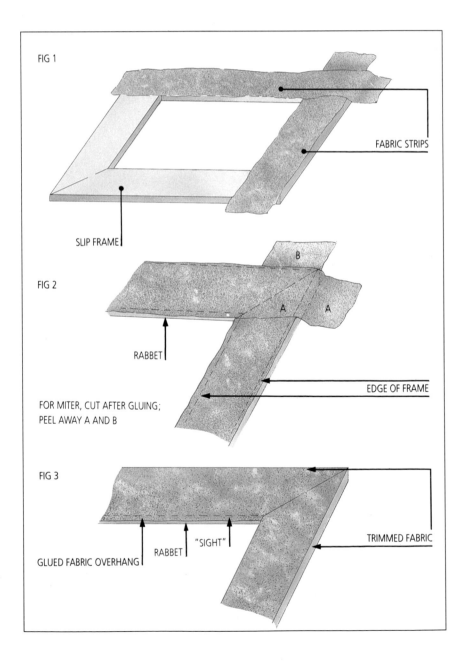

FIG 1

FABRIC STRIPS

SLIP FRAME

FIG 2

B

A   A

RABBET

EDGE OF FRAME

FOR MITER, CUT AFTER GLUING;
PEEL AWAY A AND B

FIG 3

TRIMMED FABRIC

GLUED FABRIC OVERHANG   RABBET   "SIGHT"

PREPARATION

■ The first step is to work out accurately the sizes of the inner and outer frames and, from these measurements, to calculate the amount of liner and molding needed. Measure the picture and add an allowance of ⅛in (0.3cm) for the inner frame – no allowance is needed on the outer frame.

1 Now make the inner frame following steps 1–6 for the basic mitered frame. However, if the purchased liner is made of cloth, be sure to protect it with masking tape whenever a cut is made – this keeps the cloth from tearing. Proceed as follows:

2 Replace the short pieces in their correct positions and tighten the frame clamp by pulling up the cord. When it is really tight (the cord should "ping" when pulled), secure it firmly. Wipe off any excess glue that has oozed out. Set aside to dry for a few hours. As this "frame" will be framed, you need not pin it unless it is very deep.

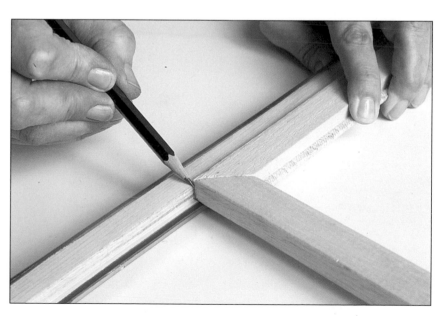

3 Now make the outer frame using the basic mitered frame directions. You can use the completed inner frame to mark the necessary measurements on the molding but do not add an allowance.

4 When this frame is complete, place the picture into the slip frame and secure with brads.

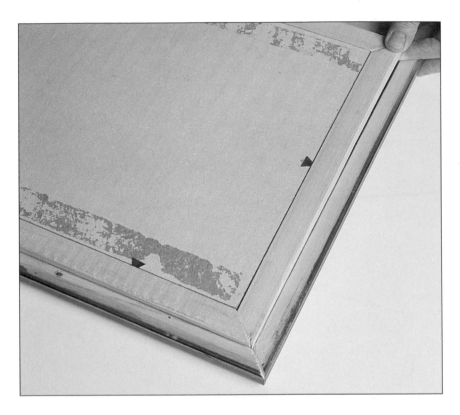

5 Place this "frame" in the outer frame. Screw eyes are normally used to hang this type of frame.

6 The slip liner adds a soft edge to the picture and separates it from the frame.

FABRIC FRAMES

SIMPLE METHOD **86**

PADDED METHOD **90**

EMBROIDERED DECORATION **94**

APPLIQUE DECORATION **95**

POCKET MIRROR **96**

SIMPLE METHOD

This frame can be made in any size depending on the size of the photograph. For larger sizes, however, the proportions may have to be altered. This frame measures 2in (5cm) more than the photograph both in length and in width. Prepare all the parts before starting.

E Q U I P M E N T

- thin card
- fabric for covering
- fusible webbing
- piece of paper for lining
- pencil
- ruler
- scissors
- craft knife
- glue
- iron
- scrap paper

FIG 1

1 Cut two pieces of thin card to the required size. Mark and cut a window in one piece leaving a 1in (2.5cm) border all around. Using the window piece, cut out the easel following the diagram (Fig. 1) as a guide. The easel should be no more than half the height of the frame.

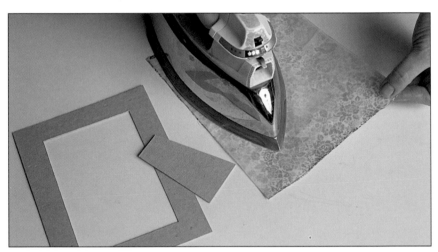

2 Cut two pieces of fabric and fusible paper-backed webbing 1½in (3.5cm) larger all around than the card frame. Then cut two pieces of fabric for the easel so they overlap the easel by 1½in (3.5cm) at the top and by ½in (1.5cm) at both sides and the wide end. Iron the webbing to the wrong side of all the fabric pieces.

3 Peel away the paper from the piece of fabric for the frame back, lay it on the corresponding piece of card and carefully iron in position. Take care not to iron over the edges because the fabric will adhere to the ironing surface.

4 To turn in the edges, use the tip of the iron. First work on the frame back. Turn in the four corners and fix down. Then turn in the sides. Pay particular attention to the corner areas to make them as neat as possible.

5 Follow the same procedure with the easel piece, but leave the 1½in (3.5cm) extension at the top free. Lay this on the other piece of easel and draw around it. Cut just inside this line, peel away the backing and iron it into position, including the extension.

6 Lay the completed easel in the center of the frame back on the fabric-covered side. At this point, you should decide whether the finished frame will be vertical (portrait) or horizontal (landscape). Holding the tab of fabric out of the way, mark the position of the top of the easel. Using the craft knife, carefully cut through the card slightly above this line.

7 Push the tab through this slit, check to make sure the easel is in the correct position, apply glue to the tab and hold down until fixed.

8 Peel away the backing paper from the remaining piece of fabric, carefully position it on top of the card for the frame front and iron in place. Cut out a smaller window ½in (1.5cm) away from card window but do not discard the fabric.

9 Turn in the outer edges as on the frame back and iron in place.

10 Now clip the excess on the window edges almost into the corners, turn this over to the wrong side and iron into place.

11 Cut the piece of paper so that it is a fraction smaller than the completed back of the frame. Glue this paper onto the wrong side of the fabric-covered back to mask the turned-in edges and tab. It will also help the photograph slide in and out of the frame easily.

12 Apply glue to three edges of the paper-covered back of the frame leaving the bottom, where the base of the easel is centered, unglued. Carefully position the frame front on top and place under a weight, such as a pile of books, to dry. If you wish, cut a piece of acetate the same size as the photograph and slide it into place with the photograph to protect it.

15 Then place the restraining strap between the easel and the frame back and hold until fixed.

FIG 2

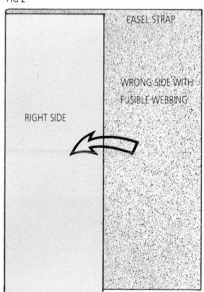

EASEL STRAP

WRONG SIDE WITH FUSIBLE WEBBING

RIGHT SIDE

13 Finally, make a restraining strap to keep the easel in place. Take a small scrap of material – 2½in (7cm) square – from the window cut-out. Peel off the paper backing, fold over one third and press with the iron tip. Fold over the remaining third and press.

FIG 3

EASEL STRAP

GLUE   GLUE

14 The strap is now ⅞in × 2½in (2cm × 6cm). Fold in half lengthwise and apply glue in a narrow line at both ends.

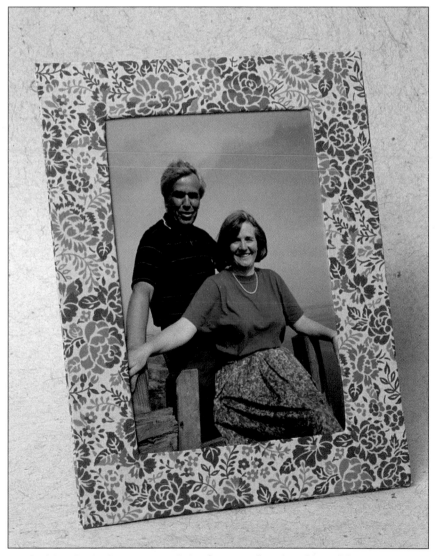

16 The fabric for the frame can match the decor or reflect the subject of the photograph.

89

PADDED METHOD

E Q U I P M E N T

- thick card
- thin card
- scrap card for templates or template plastic
- fabric for covering
- batting
- double-sided clear adhesive tape
- adhesive suitable for fabric
- pencil
- ruler
- scissors with points
- craft knife
- pins
- needle
- thread
- sandpaper or emery board
- braid or piping for trimming (optional)
- sewing machine (optional)

FIG 1   FIG 2

P R E P A R A T I O N

- Decide whether the frame opening is to be oval or circular. Then cut two pieces of thick card – square if the opening is circular, or rectangular for the oval window (see Fig. 1). Cut one piece of card for the easel (see Fig. 2).

- Make a template: draw a circle using a compass or an oval, using the method described on page 37. Cut out the window.

- Cut two pieces of fabric ¾in (2cm) larger all around than the card pieces and one piece the same size as the card to use as a facing. Also cut one piece which is ¾in (2cm) smaller all around than the card pieces; this piece can be cut from contrasting fabric. For the easel, cut two pieces 3in × 6in (8cm × 15cm). Cut two pieces of batting the same size as the card.

1 Draw around the template onto one piece of thick card.

2 Cut out the window. If the edges of the opening are rough, use the sandpaper to smooth them.

3 Apply adhesive to both pieces of card and carefully place the batting on the card. Allow to dry.

4 Then, using the pointed scissors, cut out the opening.

5 Place the card, batting side up, on the fabric piece of the same size wrong side up and draw around the opening.

6 Lay this piece of fabric, with the opening drawn on it, in the center of one of the large pieces with the right sides together. Pin in position and stitch carefully around the drawn line.

7 Cut away the fabric inside the stitching leaving a ¼in (0.5cm) seam allowance.

8 Clip almost to the stitching at regular intervals all around. Turn inside out so the right sides are facing out and press.

9 Pass the facing (the smaller piece) through the opening of the frame front so that it lies against back of the card and the larger piece of fabric covers the batting on the front.

10 Pin through the seam into the cut edge of the opening, making sure that the clipped seam allowance is on the back or card side.

11 Carefully apply some adhesive around the back of the frame close to the opening, press the seam allowance in position and allow to dry. Glue the rest of the facing in position neatly on the back.

12 Cut strips of double-sided tape and lay them along two of the outside edges of frame. Peel away the backing strips and turn in the corners. Stretching the fabric, turn over the edge and press on to the sticky tape. Now work on the opposite edge.

13 Next lay strips of double-sided tape along the other two outside edges and turn in the remaining fabric, making the corners as neat as possible. If you are using a thick fabric such as velvet, miter the corners to avoid excess bulk.

14 Take the piece of card for the back, center the smaller piece of fabric on it and glue in place. Then take the remaining large piece of fabric and cover the card as above.

FIG 3

FABRIC

BATTING

THICK CARD

DOUBLE-SIDED CLEAR ADHESIVE TAPE

SPACER

DOUBLE-SIDED CLEAR
ADHESIVE TAPE

FABRIC

BATTING

THICK CARD

LINING

15 From scrap card, cut two strips ¼in (0.5cm) wide and as long as the frame and one strip ¼in (0.5cm) wide. This strip should be long enough to fit snugly at the top of the frame between the two long strips when they are glued in position just inside the outside edges. These act as spacers.

16 If the frame is to be trimmed with lace, insert it at this point. Apply adhesive to one side of the spacers and press in position on the frame back. Apply more glue to the top face of the spacers and position the completed frame front on top of the frame back (see Fig. 3). Leave to dry under a book so that the frame is under a little pressure.

17 Now lay the easel on one of the pieces of fabric cut for it and draw around it. Place it on top of the other piece with right sides together and stitch along the two long sides and across the top. Leave the pointed end open. Trim away the excess fabric and turn right side out.

18 Take the card piece for the easel and score across the dotted line, being careful not to cut through. Push the card into the fabric case, turn in the edges on the open side and stitch together.

19 Bend the completed easel and place the pointed end in the corner of the back. Apply adhesive to the bent area and press into position.

20 Slide the picture into the frame from the bottom.

21 The padded frame has a soft look that is especially appropriate for photographs of children.

■ You can make padded frames in different shapes and sizes using remnants of dress or light furnishing fabric.

EMBROIDERED DECORATION

This frame is similar to the padded fabric frame on page 90, but it has a more elaborate shape and embroidered decoration. You can vary the shape and size of the frame if you wish. If the outer edge is curved, cut notches in the fabric so that it turns smoothly – this technique is equivalent to clipping the inside curve of the facing.

EQUIPMENT

- thin card
- fabric for covering
- fusible webbing
- piece of paper for lining
- pencil
- ruler
- scissors
- craft knife
- adhesive suitable for fabric
- iron
- scrap paper
- embroidery thread

PREPARATION

■ First design the embroidery – it can relate to the picture to be framed or it can be an unrelated design.

Remember that the design and final appearance of the frame should not overpower the picture.

1 Mark the frame area with basting stitches and decide where the embroidery should be positioned. Transfer the design to the material, using either a pencil or a washable quilter's pen, and begin to work the embroidery.

2 In this piece the stem stitch, cretan stitch and french knot were used. Several shades of green thread give depth to the leaves and the stems. If you wish, you can stretch the material on an embroidery hoop.

3 When the embroidery is completed make up the frame following the directions for the padded frame on page 90.

APPLIQUE DECORATION

This padded frame is decorated with appliqué. The method and materials used are similar to those in the previous projects. Try to choose a fabric that will complement and blend with the picture to be framed. If the frame is made from a very decorative fabric and an appliqué is added, the picture may be completely overpowered.

The only extra equipment you will need are fabric scraps for the appliqué and fusible webbing.

PREPARATION

▌ First design the appliqué – this can relate to the picture to be framed or it can be an unrelated design.

▌ Mark the frame area with basting stitches and decide where the appliqué should be positioned.

▌ Iron the fusible webbing on the wrong side of the fabric scraps. Make templates of the shapes and draw the required number of pieces on the paper side of the webbing, cut them out and peel away the backing.

2 Stitch around the edges of the shapes using a sewing machine and zig-zag stitch, if possible.

1 Position the pieces on the fabric for the frame and carefully iron into place.

3 Once decorated, the frame should be made up in the same way as the padded frame on page 90. The shape and colors of the appliqué petals clearly echo the form of the plant in the photograph.

▌ In the example shown here, the material chosen is comparatively plain – the appliqué flower matches the trim of the frame and harmonizes with the clothes worn by the child.

POCKET MIRROR

The mirror used in this project is 3in × 4in (8cm × 10cm), but you could use the same procedure to frame a smaller or larger size. If possible, have the edges of the mirror polished so that they are no longer sharp, or rub them down with emery paper.

EQUIPMENT

- thin mirror
- card
- fabric
- fusible webbing
- double-sided clear adhesive tape
- paper
- pencil
- ruler
- scissors
- craft knife

PREPARATION

- Cut a piece of card the same size as the mirror. Cut a window in this, leaving a frame of ½in (1.5cm) all around.
- Cut one piece each of fabric and fusible webbing 1in (2.5cm) larger all around than the mirror – in this case 4in × 5in (10cm × 12.5cm). Cut a second piece of each the same size as the mirror. Fuse the fabric pieces to the corresponding webbing pieces.
- Position the card frame front on the fabric and draw around the window. Draw another window ¼in (0.5cm) away within it and cut it out.

1 Peel away the paper backing from the webbing and use the iron to bond the fabric to the card frame front. Turn in and iron down the window seam allowance to the back of the card frame front.

2 Apply small pieces of double-sided tape to the window seam allowance on the frame front.

3 Peel away the tape backing and press the frame front onto the mirror.

4 Cut a piece of paper the same size as the mirror and stick it to the back with double-sided tape. Then turn in the outer fabric edges and iron to bond.

5 Now iron the remaining piece of fabric onto the back of the mirror to give a neat finish.

6 Pocket mirrors make excellent gifts.

MULTIPLE FRAMES

HINGED WOOD FRAMES **98**

MULTI-MATS **100**

DOUBLE FABRIC FRAMES **102**

HINGED WOOD FRAMES

Two or three related pictures can be framed in identical frames, and these can then be hinged together with appropriate metal hinges. In the example shown here two small posters, framed in simple molding, have been joined with small brass hinges.

EQUIPMENT

- as for basic mitered frame (see page 74)
- small brass hinges
- bradawl
- brass screws
- small screwdriver

PREPARATION

■ The method for making these frames is exactly the same as for the basic mitered frame (see page 74).

■ In making an identical pair of frames, it is a good idea to keep the pieces for each apart – it is very unlikely that the four pieces measured and cut by hand for each frame will be exactly the same.

■ When the two frames are complete, lay them side by side and decide on the position of the hinges. Placing them is done by eye – as a rough guide, divide the frame edge into quarters and place one hinge at the bottom of the top quarter and the other hinge at the top of the bottom quarter (see Fig. 1).

FIG 1

FIG 2

BACKING

ARTWORK

MAT

HINGE

GLASS

MOLDING

1 Now, using the bradawl, mark the actual position of the hinges on the first frame and screw in place. Be sure to get the hinges in the correct place on the frame molding so that the frames will open and close (see Fig. 2). To achieve this, the pin of the hinge must protrude at the front of the molding so that movement is unimpeded.

2 Stand the two frames in the closed position on a firm surface – if the bottom edges are not level, the frames will not stand properly when they are joined. With the bradawl, mark the holes for the other half of the hinge and screw together.

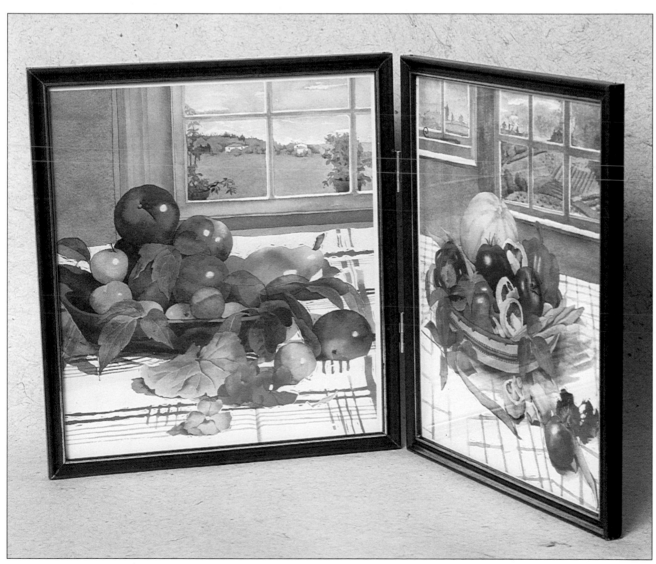

3 The hinged frames link the two pictures and make them free-standing.

MULTI-MATS

It is possible to buy ready-cut mats with one or more windows; a few examples are shown on the facing page. If these are not suitable, you can design and cut your own.

a few examples are shown on the facing page.

EQUIPMENT

- selected matting
- ruler
- pencil
- large piece of paper
- scrap paper
- circle cutter
- craft knife or scissors
- fine sandpaper
- masking tape

The photographs on this page show several generations of one family; they are matted in a simple family-tree formation to show the relationships. As the windows are quite small and show only the heads, they were cut with a circle cutter and therefore have no bevel (professional framers have machinery to cut ovals and circles with bevels). Rectangular windows in a multi-mat could be cut in the usual way.

1 This kind of project needs careful planning; use a large piece of paper to decide on the positions and then work out the overall size of the mat.

2 If the windows are all to be the same size, you can cut out a template with a window, and use it to trim the photographs.

4 When you have cut all the windows from the matting and smoothed away any slight unevenness with sandpaper, you can fix the photographs in position with masking tape.

3 Allow plenty of space and time to cut out the windows to minimize errors. You would not want to have to mark out and cut the windows more than once!

5 Here, the names were written, using calligraphy, on paper that harmonizes with the matting and glued beneath the appropriate photograph to give an overall unity to the piece.

6 All the faces, names and relationships show clearly in the finished picture.

READY-CUT MULTI-MATS

The postcards displayed in this nine-window mat came from various places, but they are all related. Framed together, they show an interesting and slightly unusual use of this type of mat.

1 Multi-mats come in a variety of sizes and have differing numbers of windows.

2 Select the mat that comes closest to your needs – in this case one with many windows of various shapes for the different types of pictures to be framed.

3 Each picture was fitted to the most appropriately sized and shaped window to make a balanced whole.

101

DOUBLE FABRIC FRAMES

This double, free-standing padded frame is made in almost the same way as the basic padded frame (see page 90).

EQUIPMENT

- thick card
- thin card
- scrap card for templates or template plastic
- fabric for covering
- fusible webbing and interfacing
- batting
- double-sided clear adhesive tape
- adhesive suitable for fabric
- pencil
- ruler
- scissors with points
- craft knife
- pins, needle and thread
- sandpaper or emery board
- braid or piping for trimming (optional)
- sewing machine (optional)

PREPARATION

▮ Begin by preparing all the materials. Cut four pieces of card to the required size; two of these will need windows. You will also need a narrow (½in – 1.5cm) strip of card the same length as the frame.

▮ Cut two pieces of fabric to cover the fronts and two pieces as backing for the two frame fronts – the backs can contrast if you wish. Cut the batting for the frame fronts at this stage.

▮ The fabric for the outside of the frame should be twice the width of one frame as it covers both frames (see Fig. 1). The outside could be made from the same contrasting fabric you use to back the frame fronts.

▮ A hinge piece is also required – this should be the same length as the frame and 2½in (7cm) wide. One piece of fusible interfacing and one piece of fusible webbing should be cut to this size.

FIG 1

1 Make the two frame fronts as for the basic padded frame (see page 90).

2 Take the piece of fusible interfacing and mark the center. Lay the strip of card on this line. Draw lines ½in (1.5cm) away from the strip on both sides. Position the two frame backs against these lines with the interfacing on top of the card. Iron in place. Lay the card strip in the center of the interfacing and iron.

3 Now measure this hinged piece and cut a piece of batting to fit. Glue it to the outside.

4 Trim away the excess batting — the interfacing should still be visible.

5 Next cover the frame back using double-sided adhesive tape. Take particular care with the center hinged area. Turn in the top and bottom edges first; then turn in the sides making sure not to pull them so tight that the frame will not close.

6 Take the piece of webbing and iron it onto the fabric piece of the same size.

7 Peel away the backing and fuse in place down the center of the frame to cover the card hinge.

8 Now glue the small pieces of backing fabric in place on the hinged frame back.

9 Complete the frame as for the basic padded frame, following steps 15 and 16 (see page 92).

10 The openings in these frames should be along the central edges close to the hinge.

11 The completed frame links the two photographs and enables them to stand.

BOX
FRAMES

WOODEN FRAMES **106**

ACRYLIC FRAMES **110**

FLOATING AND PLATFORM FRAMES **112**

WOODEN FRAMES

Some pieces of work to be framed are three dimensional. There are several ways to deal with this challenge – some are more complicated than others.

First, consider the depth of the object to be framed. Some embroidery, for example, could be accommodated by the addition of foam board or a double or triple mat (see pages 38 and 41).

If the object is deeper, you might use two frames and place the glass between them (see Fig. 1). The inner frame, for the object, could be made from a slip-style molding such as the one used for the landscape painting on page 82. The outer frame, with a deeper rabbet, would hold the glass,

the inner frame and the backing board with the object mounted on it. This method works well, but it can be expensive as it means making and paying for two frames. Also, moldings with deep rabbets can be hard to find. You can make these quite easily, however, from half-round molding and batten strips. These should be glued together and taped while drying (see Fig. 2).

A cheaper way to frame a three-dimensional object is to make a box for it and then frame the box. Various decisions need to be made before starting this type of project:

1 How will the work be fixed to the backing board? Some items, such as stones or paper or dried flowers could be glued; medals could be pinned or attached with Velcro for easy removal.
2 Will the backing board be lined? If so, this can be done with material or paper.

FIG 2

3 Is a mat required? If so, cut in the normal way and then place on top of the box and accommodate within the frame in the usual way.

EQUIPMENT

- thick cardboard or wooden strips (see below)
- frame molding
- backing board
- hardboard
- mat (optional)
- lining (optional)
- impact adhesive for cardboard or adhesive suitable for wood
- tools to make a basic mitered frame (see page 74)

PREPARATION

▌ The size of the work to be framed will determine whether cardboard or wood strips should be used for the box. If the piece is larger than 8in × 10in (20cm × 30cm) it is probably wiser to use wood.

▌ Decide on the size of the box and cut two strips of your chosen material the exact width and two strips the length, minus two thicknesses of wood or card (see Fig. 3). Cut the cardboard for the base to size.

▌ The following project uses a cardboard box lined with dark velvet to offset the piece of silver jewelry. The sloping panels are not essential, but they create shallower planes to which a lining, such as velvet, can be attached.

FIG 1

OUTER FRAME

INNER FRAME

GLASS

SPACE

MAT FOR OBJECT

BACKING

FIG 3

1 Stick the two shorter strips to the corresponding sides of the base, using the appropriate adhesive. Then stick the remaining two strips in position on the other two sides of the base. The box is now finished. If using wooden strips, secure with small brads as well, if wished.

2 Draw a rectangle in the base of the box to define the flat area where the piece of jewelry will lie. Take a piece of card to fit the width of the box and lay it against the line and touching the top edge of the box – this will give the depth of the card. Cut two pieces this size.

3 Now cut two more pieces the same depth but this time the length of the box. Place each panel, in turn, in position against the line drawn in the base in the box and mark each corner point. Cut from these marks to the top corner edges.

107

4 Stick the four panels in position.

5 Cut a piece of velvet almost twice the size of the box. Apply glue sparingly to the card and, starting from the center, stick the velvet in position. The natural give in the material will accommodate the slopes.

6 Trim away the material so that there is just enough to stick down along the outside edges of the box. Cut the corners neatly.

7 Make a basic mitered frame using the deep molding. Make sure the allowance on the frame molding is not forgotten when cutting as the velvet will take up some space. When gluing deep moldings it is helpful to use two frame clamps while the glue is drying.

8 Center the piece of jewelry in the box and pierce two holes through the velvet and cardboard close to the fixing point. Thread a short piece of brass wire through one hole, wrap around the fixing on the back of the jewelry, and return to the back of the box and twist several times.

9 Place the glass on top of the box with the jewelry fixed securely. Lower the frame carefully into position. Turn over and tape the box and frame together as usual.

109

ACRYLIC FRAMES

A quicker and simpler way to frame a small, three-dimensional piece of work is to purchase a ready-made acrylic box frame and adapt it to accommodate the piece. This might be embroidery, coins, origami or anything that is half the thickness of the frame or less. If the work is deeper, one of the other methods described should be used to ensure that the piece can be fixed firmly enough to hold it.

You can sometimes buy acrylic frames that have an insert especially designed to provide a space (see Fig. 1). The standard acrylic box frame is shown in Fig. 2. If the first frame is not available, a standard frame can be converted as follows:

EQUIPMENT

- acrylic box frame
- pencil
- metal ruler
- craft knife or scalpel
- mediumweight card
- adhesive suitable for card

PREPARATION

- Remove the existing card insert from the frame.
- Take the internal measurements of the frame as accurately as you can. Draw a rectangle of this size onto the card, less an allowance for the thickness of the card.
- Decide on the depth you need for the work to be framed. Add this measurement to each side of the rectangle.
- Now add glue flaps to the edges (see Fig. 3).

FIG 1

BOX-LIKE INSERT

ACRYLIC BOX FRAME

SPACE

FIG 2

ACRYLIC BOX FRAME

BOX-LIKE INSERT

FIG 3   GLUE FLAPS A TO POSITIONS B

1 Cut out this shape. Score all the dashed lines by ruling along them with the back of the knife.

2 Now measure the overall size of the frame and cut a piece of card this size. Cut at least two finger holes so you will be able to pull it away from the acrylic.

3 Bend all the scored lines; apply adhesive to the side flaps and glue in position.

4 Apply glue to the outer, and larger, flaps and position the box centrally on the piece of card – there will be a small overlap all around which will stop the insert from sliding too far into the frame.

5 Fix the work to be framed to a piece of card and then fix this on the box insert with double-sided clear adhesive tape or glue and place in the frame. You can add a mat supported by strips of foam board if you wish.

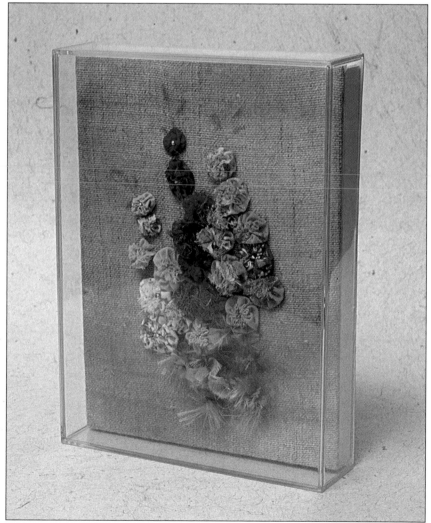

6 The box shape leaves plenty of room for the work to float; the clear frame lets in light and enhances the work's three-dimensional quality.

FLOATING AND PLATFORM FRAMES

Sometimes you may wish to frame a piece of work so that it appears to float instead of being enclosed in a frame. There are three main ways to achieve this effect:

1 Sandwich the artwork between two sheets of glass and use clips or tape to hold the pieces together. This shows both the back and front of the work.

2 Frame the work with a molding that creates a visible groove between the image and the edge of the frame (see Figs. 1a and b). The groove should appear dark to strengthen the illusion of floating; the inside edge of the molding may need to be painted a dark color.

3 Mount the work in such a way that it appears to float on the surface of the backing and then frame the whole (see Fig. 2).

The last two methods are only suitable for works that do not need to be protected from exposure to light and air as they are unglazed and, usually, unsealed.

   In the example shown here, the third method is used.

EQUIPMENT

- batten
- sheet of wood
- covering fabric
- staple gun and staples
- screws
- hand drill
- screwdriver
- wood adhesive
- molding
- tools to make a basic mitered frame (see page 74)

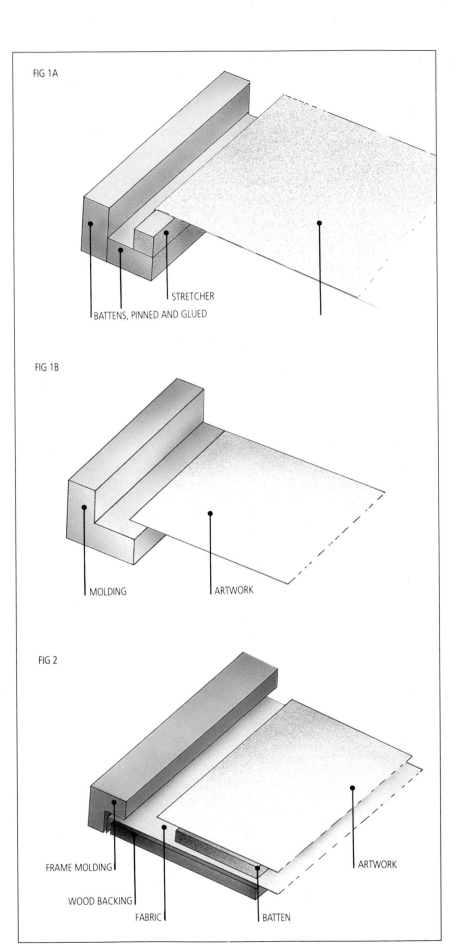

FIG 1A

STRETCHER

BATTENS, PINNED AND GLUED

FIG 1B

MOLDING   ARTWORK

FIG 2

FRAME MOLDING

WOOD BACKING

FABRIC   BATTEN

ARTWORK

MAKING THE BACKING BOARD

1 Cut two strips of batten about 2½in (7cm) shorter than the width of the picture and glue them to the back of the picture, 1in (2.5cm) from the top and the bottom and equidistant from the sides.

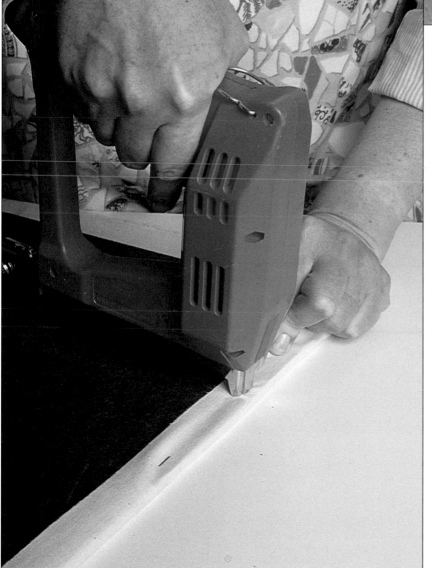

2 Next cut the sheet of wood to the required size and cover it with the fabric. Here, the wood is 20in × 16in (50cm × 40cm) and the fabric is muslin which harmonizes with the background of the painting. The fabric has been tightly stretched and stapled to the back of the wood.

3 Tuck in the corners and staple as neatly as possible.

SECURING THE ARTWORK

With the fabric side down, position the picture on the wood and calculate the position of the holes to secure it, by measuring the distance from the lower edge of the wood to the lower edge of the picture. Add the 1in (2.5cm) to the lower edge of the batten and add half the width of the batten. This gives the position for the lower holes – one in the center and one at each end. The upper holes should be marked in the same way.

3 Position the picture on the covered surface of the wood and screw through from the back to secure it using flat-head screws.

4 Now make a mitered frame for this "picture" in the usual way (see page 74). It will not be necessary to cut glass for this frame or to seal the back. The picture is fixed into the frame with hardboard corners on the back because the molding has a narrow rabbet; the fabric-covered board fits flush into it allowing no space for brads.

1 Drill the holes through the wood and mark these with a nail on the battens. Then drill guide holes into the battens to receive the screws.

2 Countersink the drill holes so that the wall is not damaged by protruding screws once the picture is hung.

5 This oil painting had been worked on a rough piece of wood in a spontaneous way; a conventional frame would have hemmed it in and would not have extended the feeling of space inherent in the painting.

READY-MADE
FRAMES

METAL FRAMES **116**

WOODEN FRAMES **118**

CLIP FRAMES **120**

METAL FRAMES

Metal frames in a variety of sizes and finishes are now available in many shops; they can also be ordered in special sizes.

The photo-collage shown here has a very simple red metal frame which complements the piece of work. As it is a very large piece measuring 32in × 44in(81cm × 112cm), glass would have made the frame excessively heavy. The glass-substitute used instead is much lighter in weight, but it is easily scratched and attracts static. In price, they are about the same.

If the metal frame comes unassembled, a pack containing all components needed to assemble it will be supplied. This will contain corner pieces, screws, clips to keep the backing in position and hangers. The glass, or glass-substitute if you want to use it, and the backing must be purchased separately. You may be able to order them from the frame supplier.

Gather together all the parts of the frame, the piece to be framed, a mat if you are using one, and the wire. The only equipment you will need is a screwdriver and a pair of pliers.

1 Take one short piece of the frame and two corner pieces, slide them into position and screw up but do not tighten.

2 Take the two long pieces of the frame and slide them into position at right angles to the short piece with the corner brackets. Screw up these corners checking to make sure the miters are as neat as possible before tightening.

3 Take the second short piece, insert the other two corner pieces and screw up but do not tighten. Leave on one side. If using glass, clean the inside. If using glass-substitute, peel away the protective covering from both sides. With the frame flat and front side down, slide the glass or substitute into position.

4 Next, slide the piece of work, with its mat if used, into position, image side down. Finally, slide the backing into the frame. If the hangers are of the sliding type, put them in at this stage but do not tighten.

5 Take the remaining short piece, with the attached corner pieces and slip into place on the frame. Making sure that all the layers – glass, picture and backing – are in the groove, screw up and tighten.

6 Place the spring clips evenly around the back of the frame to keep everything firmly in place.

7 Secure the hangers in position approximately one quarter to one third of the way down the frame and attach the picture wire.

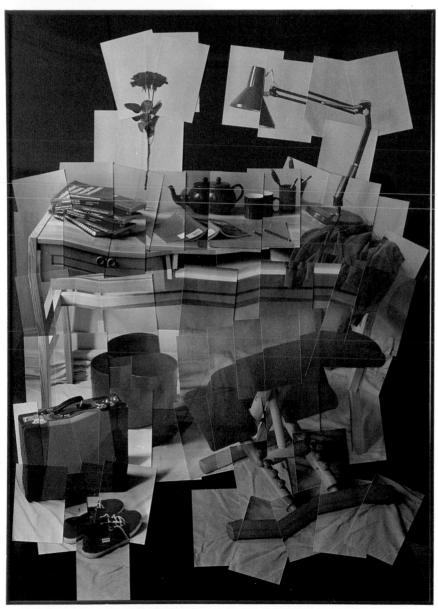

8 The metal frame adds a narrow border and is an easy option for a simple frame.

117

WOODEN FRAMES

A large selection of ready-made wooden frames is available; several alternatives are shown here. These frames can be useful, but the range of sizes available in ordinary shops tends to be limited.

If you want a large or unusual size, go to a specialist framing shop where you will have a greater choice and can order the size you need.

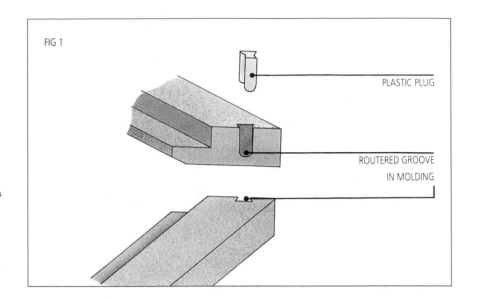

FIG 1

PLASTIC PLUG

ROUTERED GROOVE
IN MOLDING

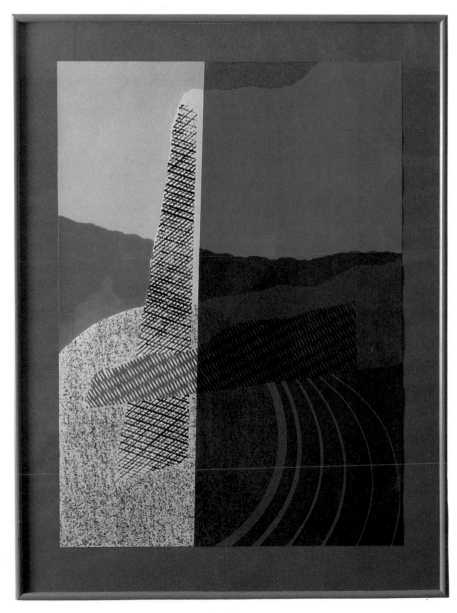

■ The silkscreen print shown here needed very careful framing because of its vibrant colors. It is printed right to the edge of the paper and has therefore been matted on a larger piece of background paper to emphasize the technique. The blue molding is perfect for the picture and shows that color is as important as shape when choosing a frame.

The most modern way to put together a wooden frame is to use plastic plugs to join miters which have been shaped to form a type of dovetail joint (see Fig. 1). Some professional framers now use this method in addition to the traditional underpinned method.

When choosing ready-made frames make sure to have the artwork on hand so you can choose a frame that will show both picture and frame to their best advantage.

■ Ready-made wooden frames come in a wide variety of finishes to go with almost any decor; some include mats. This selection features painted, veneered and antique-gold finishes.

CLIP FRAMES

Clip frames are probably the cheapest of all ready-made frames and, if properly used, can look extremely attractive. They come in a vast number of sizes and in several styles.

Sometimes a piece of artwork can be sandwiched in place in a clip frame and hung. If you want to embellish the artwork, however, choose a clip frame at least one size larger than necessary and mat the work in one of the ways described in the chapter on Mat Board Frames (see page 27).

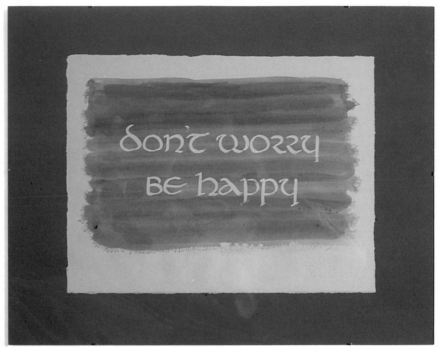

3 Clip frames allow a very clean, uncluttered effect.

1 This piece of calligraphy has a lovely deckled edge which would be hidden if it was matted in the usual way. For this reason the piece was mounted on a piece of matting that harmonizes.

2 The mounted artwork is then sandwiched in the clip frame.

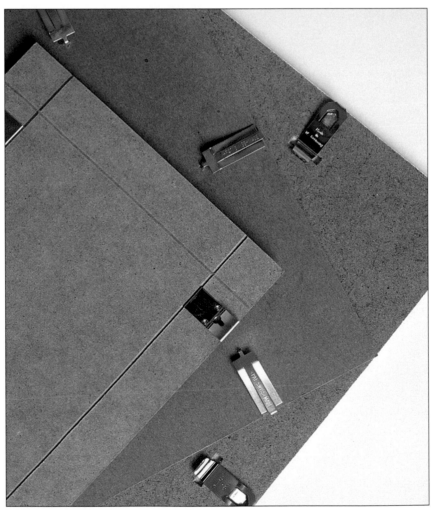

■ A number of different type of clips can be used to hold the clear front of the frame to the backing. Some are shown here.

APPENDIX

HISTORY OF PICTURE FRAMING **122**

GLOSSARY **124**

INDEX **126**

ACKNOWLEDGMENTS **128**

THE HISTORY OF PICTURE FRAMING

In prehistoric times pictures did not have frames – people painted directly onto the walls of their cave dwellings. Even when ancient civilizations began to construct free-standing buildings they continued to decorate the walls. One

Above These cave paintings in Tanzania are thought to date from after the prehistoric period, but are typical in that their creators chose to depict scenes from everyday life – hunting, the ever-important search for food, being a predominant subject. Not bounded within a frame, the images almost appear as a moving tableau.

form of wall painting, the fresco, was made on wet plaster.

For centuries, paintings – usually religious works – were painted directly onto wood panels and remained unframed. In medieval times a decorative border was sometimes added to the picture. The

illuminated borders, painstakingly crafted by monks to enclose pages of beautifully lettered text, are one example.

The first recorded frames appeared in about the 13th century and were made to enclose religious works. They were made for churches and cathedrals, usually by the same craftsmen who designed and made the pulpits and choir stalls. These works often took the form of a triptych – three panels of wood hinged together. The central panel held the main painting and the two side panels contained a design or painting complimentary to it. As most early frames were designed to "house" pictures which were grandiose and ecclesiastical, they frequently used architectural elements. One popular style, the Tabernacle frame, incorporated pilasters and half columns.

In the 15th century, the Renaissance in Italy brought great changes in art and framing. Painters began to see themselves as artists in their own right rather than as their employers' servants, and they saw the frame as an important element in the pictures they were creating. Frames also became a practical necessity for transporting paintings (frequently portraits which were particularly popular at this time) commissioned by wealthy patrons. As artists became more respected and busier, they had less time to make their own frames; this task passed to the apprentice under the direction of the painter. In this way, the separate craft of framing came into being.

The changes that began in Italy spread to other parts of Europe, but each country developed its own style. Although carved frames still predominated, decorative finishes such as marbling, gilding and even the use of fabrics such as silk were incorporated.

Under strong French influence in

the 17th century, frames became the province of designers rather than artists. Paintings were seen as part of the interior decoration, and furniture designers became the major frame-makers; again, each country developed its own style. Many frames were mass-produced and some of the individuality was lost. But the standard of work remained high.

In the late 17th and early 18th centuries, frames became increasingly ornate, first in the Baroque style and then the Rococo style. Making these elaborate frames required a high degree of skill, and cabinet-makers contracted the work out to specialist carvers. Gradually, the popularity of these extravagant styles waned, and there was a return to simpler, more austere frames. Towards the end of the 18th century, geometric moldings again became fashionable. At this time, the Adam brothers were at work in England and their style became a major influence. Once again the frame was seen as an integral part of the picture and was specially designed to enhance it.

At the beginning of the 19th century "composition" frames were introduced, and they began to replace traditional carved wood frames. Once the technique had been mastered, composition frames could be produced much more quickly and less expensively than individually carved frames. Another new technique involved plaster moldings applied to wood bases, but this was not always successful as the plaster tended to flake off over a period of time. This technique did enable frame-makers to copy old frames more easily, however, and during the 19th century many old frames were copied heralding a return to more ornate styles.

Towards the end of the 19th century, artists again became extremely interested in the way their works were displayed. They looked upon the frame as an important part of

the whole, and this attitude continues to the present. At the same time, many interior designers today like to present art as part of the decor and they choose pictures to blend with the whole rather than for their own merit. An interesting development at present is the upsurge in value of old frames; some bring more at auction than the pictures they contain.

The history of picture framing, like so much else in history, is cyclical; styles come and go, and return again. This brief synopsis may help you to identify different styles – in museums, art galleries or auction rooms – and to assess your own pictures and frames with a little more understanding.

Above *Madonna and Child*, Duccio di Buoninsegna. Painted in tempera on a white gesso ground, with lavish application of gold leaf, this triptych is typical of religious works of the 15th century. Note that the painted sections of the wooden panels are slightly recessed and are effectively 'framed' by the raised edges.

Left This modern abstract screenprint required a simple, modern frame and the choice of colour, size and mounting materials serve to enhance the whole.

GLOSSARY

Acid-free: This term describes matting and card that do not contain acid. Acid can damage paper and, if used in framing materials, can transfer to the artwork. Acid-free matting should have an alkaline pH content of 7.5 to 9.5.

Acrylic: A rigid plastic in sheet form which is sometimes used instead of glass in picture frames. It is lighter than glass and unbreakable, but it does scratch easily.

Architrave: A type of molding used mainly around doors and windows.

Batten: A thin strip of wood used to cover joints or to provide a surface for fixing tiles.

Beading: A narrow strip of shaped material, usually wood, that is used for edging.

Bevel: A sloped edge, often used along the edge of a window in a mat.

Block mount: A piece of wood or blockboard on which a piece of artwork has been mounted.

Box frame: A deep frame designed to display a three-dimensional piece of work.

Bradawl: A pointed hand tool used to pierce wood so that screws or brads can be inserted more easily.

Clip frame: A simple frame consisting of a sheet of glass, a piece of hardboard, and special clips to hold them together. The artwork is sandwiched between the two layers.

Cold mounting: A method of fixing a piece of artwork to a backing using a spray adhesive. It is also known as wet mounting.

Conservation board: Matting made from rag pulp or from specially treated acid- and chemical-free wood pulp. It is used in the framing of valuable pieces of artwork.

Double mats: Two mats used together to give a more decorative effect. The top mat has a larger window than the lower mat. This technique is also used to provide a deeper space for work that is slightly raised.

Dry mounting: A method of fixing a piece of artwork to a backing by inserting a special film between them and applying heat. The heat causes the film to dissolve and the two layers to adhere. This process is also known as hot mounting.

Easel: An addition to the back of a frame that acts as a support and allows the frame to be free-standing.

Fillet: A strip of wood or plastic which is sometimes used to make space between a piece of art and the glass covering it. Occasionally, it is used purely for decoration. It can also be placed between the liner (see below) and the art.

Floating frame: A method of framing a piece of art, usually an oil painting, so that it appears to float against the background. This is done by creating a recess between the painting and the frame.

Glass: The glass most suitable for picture frames is $1/12$in thick. Non-reflective glass has a finely dimpled surface and is more expensive.

Glass cutter: A special tool for cutting glass. There are two types available: one has a steel wheel; the other has a diamond tip.

Glaze: To cover with glass or to apply a layer of varnish.

Gouache: Opaque watercolor paint in which the pigments are bound with glue. The lighter tones are extended with white. This medium is traditionally used for colored washes on decorative mats.

Hinge mat: The traditional way to mat an original piece of work on paper – the window mat is fixed to the backing with a paper hinge; the artwork is fixed to the backing.

Hot mounting: See dry mounting.

Liner: Another name for a slip liner (see below).

Liming wax: A special white paste mix which gives a "limed" effect when rubbed into wood. It is particularly effective on oak and on stained, open-textured wood moldings.

Marbling: The process of decorating paper or wood to resemble the mottled appearance of marble. Marbled papers may be used to decorate mats.

Marquetry: A pattern of inlaid veneers of wood. Moldings with this form of decoration can be purchased.

Mat: A piece of card surrounding a picture. It can protect and enhance the work and has many variations.

Miter: A right-angle joint or join formed by two pieces of molding (or card or fabric), each cut at a 45° angle. This type of joint is most often used in picture framing.

Miter box: A wooden or metal guide to aid in the cutting of wood for mitered corners.

Molding: A decoratively shaped strip of wood or other material. Moldings made for framing have a rabbet to hold the glass, artwork and backing, but builders' moldings can be used if a rabbet is added.

Origami: The art of paper folding. It originated in Japan.

Quadrant: A strip of wood shaped like a quarter of a circle that is used to form a rabbet.

Rabbet: The step or recess in the back of a piece of molding into which all the parts of the picture are fitted.

Ruling pen: A pen with two parallel, adjustable blades. These are filled with ink or watercolor and used to draw decorative lines on mats. Some mechanical pens of a fixed width can be purchased.

Score: To mark a line on glass or card with a cutting tool. Scoring glass allows it to be severed; scoring card allows it to be bent neatly. Neither material is cut through when scoring.

Screw eyes: Screws with a ring at the top. They are attached to the back of a frame; the wire from which the picture will hang is tied to them.

Sight: The part of the picture that is visible from the front of the frame.

Slip liner: An inner frame, usually made of wood and placed between the art work and the outer frame or molding. It is usually decorative, often covered in fabric and acts in much the same way as a mat.

Stretcher: A wooden frame to which the canvas, usually of an oil painting, is tautly tacked before it is framed.

Veneer: A thin layer of good quality wood laid over an inferior base. Veneers are often used to make decorative inlays.

Wash: A thin coating of diluted paint used to obtain a transparent or delicate finish.

Wash line: A wash applied in a band between inked or painted lines.

Wet mounting: A method of fixing a piece of artwork to a backing using a spray adhesive.

Window: The hole cut in the mat through which the artwork is visible.

INDEX

A

acetate
for protection 65, 88
for stencils 23
acid-free backing card and paper 8–9, 28, 124
acid-free glue 28
acid-free matting 8–9, 28, 124
acrylic 125
acrylix box frames 110–111
acrylic paintings: slip liners 82
adhesive tape, double-sided clear 14–15, 46
angles see curves and angles
appliqué decoration, padded fabric frame 95
"architraves" 124
artwork not completely flat see three-dimensional items

B

backing board (hardboard) 8–9, 80
for box frames 106
backing card and paper, acid-free 8–9, 28, 124
battens 56–7, 124
beading 124
bevel-cut mats see mats, bevel-cut
"bevels" 124
birch plywood cutout frames 61–70
bits for drill 12–13
black core matting 8–9
black and white artwork, straight-cut mats 30–1, 35
block mounts 124
borders
from battens 56–7, 124
from wallpaper 73
of medieval pictures 122
box frames 105–14, 124
bradawls 12–13, 124
butt-jointed wooden frames 72–3

C

calligraphy, in clip frames 120
card frames, folded 20–1
card and paper for backing, acid-free 8–9, 28, 124
cards, with slits 18
carved frames 122–3
center of picture (visual cf geometrical) 28
child photographs: padded fabric frames 93
child's drawings: decorated folded frames 23
circle cutters 14–15
circular openings, fabric frames 90
circular windows, multi-mats 100–01
clamps
G-clamps 62–5
miter 12–13, 75
clay frames 58–60
clip frames and clips 16, 120, 124
coins, in acrylic box frame 110
cold mounting 124
collages 29
photo-collage 116–7
see also postcards and small pictures (sets)
color
cards with slits 18
decorated folded frames 22–3

color of mount 28
sets of small pictures 40
shown through cutout designs 43
V-cut and double-bevel mats 42–3
compass 14–15
"composition" frames (plaster and resin) 123
conservation quality matting 8–9, 28, 124
corner gauges 14–15
substitute 44
corners
folded corners and backing (lightweight frame) 26
photo-corners for securing picture 20
corners of window, cutting and neatening 31
craft knife 14–15
curves and angles (for particular effects) 43
shaped outline 69–70
fabric padded frame 94
shaped window 68, 69–70
see also circular; oval
cutout designs in mat 43
cutout frames
card or paper 19
wood 61–70
cutout paper decorations 67
cutting mats 14–15
not for bevel-angled cuts 32

D

D-rings 16, 80
decorated folded frames 22–3
decorative mats: lines and washes 44–5, 46, 125
découpage finish 67
"distancing" picture 28, 82
double frames
hinged padded fabric 102–4
hinged wood 98–9
double mats 40–1, 47, 124
double-bevel mats 42–3
double-window mats 40
drill bits 12–13
dry mounting 124

E

easel hinges 16
easels (for free-standing frame) 18, 19, 48–50, 125
embroidered pictures see fabric pictures
embroidered decoration, padded fabric frame 94
envelopes, for mailing framed photographs 20
environment see surroundings
equipment and tools 6, 7–16, 28
accessories 16
see also specific projects

F

fabric covering 123
floating frames 112–14
mitered frames 82–4
mats 36–7
slip liners 125
fabric frames 85–96
padded 90–6
double 102–4
simple 86–9
fabric lining, for box frames 106–9
fabric-covered matting 8–9
fabric pictures (embroidery; patchwork; tapestry) 36, 72, 106, 110
family tree multi-mat frames 100–01

color of mount 28
felt-tip pens 14–15, 44–5
fillets (strips of wood or plastic) 46, 47, 124
finishes
painted wooden frames 62–5, 69–70, 72–3, 122–3
ready-made 119
stained wood frames 66, 68, 72–7
finishes for moldings 10, 11
flecked matting 8–9
"floating" frames 111, 112–14, 124
flowers, paper or dried: in box frames 106
foam, polystyrene
for mats with extra depth 38
for padded effect 36
folded card frames 20–1
decorated 22–3
folded corners and backing (lightweight frame) 26
frame stands 16, 48–9
frameless pictures 28, 122
clip frames and clips 16, 120, 124
frames within frames (mitered frames with slip liners) 82–4, 106
free-standing frames 18, 19
easels 10, 18, 19, 48–50, 125
hinged 98–9
double fabric frames 102–4
medieval triptyches 122, 123
fret saws 62–5

G

G-clamps 62–5
gesso frames 123
glass 78–9, 124
artwork protected by mat 28
items sandwiched between two sheets 112
non-reflective 124
two frames with glass in rabbet 106
unglazed items 72, 82, 112–14
glass cutters 12–13, 78, 124
glass substitutes
acrylic 125
acrylic box frames 110–11
for large metal frames 116–7
"glaze" 124
glaziers' points 16
glue, acid-free 28
glue pen 14–15
gold adhesive tape 46, 47
gold finishes (incl. gilding) 6, 11, 119, 123
gold marker pens, for lines 45
gouache 125
gummed hangers 19
gummed hooks, for lightweight frames 18, 23
gummed tape 14–15

H

hand planes 12–13
hangers
gummed 16, 19
plastic self-adhesive 16
triangle 16
hardboard for backing 80
box frames 106
hardboard for mounts 8–9
heavy items (eg tiles), butt-jointed wooden frames 72–3
hinged- double-, padded fabric frames 102–4
hinged wooden frames 98–9
triptyches 122, 123
hinges
acid-free 28
easel 16
hooks, gummed: for lightweight frames 18, 23
hot (or dry) mounting 124

I

Ingres matting 8–9
inks
for lines and washes 44
ruling pens 125
sponged-on, for decorated folded frame 22–3
inlays 125
inserts, in acrylic box frames 110
inserts (slip liners) 125
with mitered frame 82–4, 106

J

jewelry, in box frames 106–9
jointed wooden frames 72–7, 119
butt-jointed 72–3
miter-jointed 74–7, 125
slip liners 82–4, 106

K

keyhole board 62–5

L

lace-trimmed fabric padded frames 92
large fabric frames 86
large metal frames 116–7
large miter-jointed wooden frames 75
large ready-made wooden frames 118
lightweight frames 17–26
liming wax 125
linen matting 8–9
liners see slip liners
lines and washes to decorate mat 44–5, 46
ruling pen 125

M

marbling 123, 125
marquetry 125
mat cutters 14–15
materials see tools and equipment
mats
bevel-cut 30, 32–3, 124
decorated with colored adhesive tape 46
double-bevel 42–3
cutout designs 43
decorated 44–5, 46, 125
double and triple 40–1, 47, 124
double-window 40
with extra depth 38–9
covering with fabric 36
fabric-covered 36–7
multi-mats 100–01
paper-covered 34–5
straight-cut 30–1
V-cut 42–3
matting and mounting 8–9, 28, 124
mat board frames 27–50
medals: in box frames 106
metal frames, ready-made 116–7
mirror clips 16
mirror frames
padded fabric 96
papier-mâché 52–5
miter box 12–13
miter clamp 12–13
miter joints 125
in wooden frames 74–7
slip liners 82–4, 106
moldings 10, 11, 74–7, 123, 125
architraves 124
multi-cutters, for cutting strips 46
multi-mats 100–01
multi-screwdrivers 12–13
multiple frames 97–104
sets of tiles, etc, butt-jointed wooden frames 72–3

triptyches 122, 123
see also postcards and small pictures
(sets)

N

nail punches 12–13
nail sets 12–13

O

oil paintings, unglazed
"floating" in box frame 112–4
slip liners 82
old masters 6, 122–3
optical illusions 28
"distancing" picture from frame 82
strips of colored paper for double
mat effect 40–1
"origami" 125
origami items, in acrylic box frame 110
origami picture frames 24–5
oval openings, fabric frames 90–3
oval windows
fabric-covered mats 37
folded card frames 20–1

P

padded fabric frames 90–6
appliqué decoration 95
double 102–4
embroidered decoration 94
pocket mirror 96
padded fabric mats 36
painted frames
papier-mâché 51–7
wooden 62–5, 69–70, 72–3, 122–3
ready-made 119
paints and paint brushes 14–15, 125
lines and washes 44–5, 46, 125
paper
covering mats with decorative
paper 34–5
cutout paper decorations 67
strips of colored paper,
for illusion of double mat 40–1
to decorate mat 46–7
wallpaper border for butt-jointed
frame 73
paper and card for backing, acid-free
8–9, 28, 124
papier-mâché mirror frames 52–5
papier-mâché picture frames 52, 56–7
pencils 14–15
pens
felt-tip 14–15, 44–5
gold marker pens 45
ruling pens 125
photo-collages 116–7
photo-corners, for folded card frames
20
photo-mounts, for folded card frames
20
photographs
family tree multi-mat frames 100–
101
folded card frames 20–1
picture glass cf window glass 78
picture wire 16
planes: hand planes 12–13
plaster frames 123
plastic
acrylic (rigid plastic) 125
acrylic box frames 110–11
template plastic for stencils 23
plastic plugs 119
plastic slip fillets 46, 47, 124
platform frames 112–14
pliers 12–13
plywood cutout frames 61–70
pocket mirror 96
polystyrene foam

for mats with extra depth 38
for padded effect 36
postcards and small pictures
cards with slits 18
frames with folded corners and
backing 26
origami picture frames 24–5
sets,
double-window mats 40
ready-cut multi-mats 101
visually united with lines on mat
44–5
see also multiple frames
prints (framed), lines and washes on
mat 44–5
proportions for correct balance 6, 18,
28

Q

quadrant 125

R

rabbets (in moldings) 125
"raising the grain" (of plywood frame)
62
rapidographs, for lines on mat 45
ready-cut multi-mats 101
ready-made frames
acrylic box 110–11
clip 120
metal 116–7
wooden 118–9
religious items, in history 122
rings and clips 16, 80
ruling pens 125

S

sanding plywood surface 62
saws and sawing 75
fret saws 62–5
tenon saws 12–13
scissors 14–15
scoring 125
screenprints in frame 118, 123
screw eyes 16, 84, 125
screw rings 16, 81
screwdrivers 12–13
sepia pictures 66, 67
set squares, metal 14–15
sets of postcards and small pictures,
see under postcards
sets of tiles, etc, butt-jointed wooden
frames 72–3
shapes *see* circular; curves and angles;
ovals
"sight" (of picture) 125
silk, on frames 123
slip fillets, plastic 46, 47, 124
slip liners 125
with mitered frame 82–4, 106
slits: cards with slits 18
small pictures *see* postcards and small
pictures
"space" around the picture 28
sponged-on ink, for decorated folded
frame 22–3
squares: try squares 12–13
stained wood frames 66, 68, 72–7
stands, for finished frames 16, 48–9
stenciled designs
decorated folded frames 23
papier-mâché frames 52, 56–7
stones, in box frames 106
straight-cut mats 30–1
stretchers 125
strips of colored paper for double and
triple mats 40–1
strips of colored paper or tape, to
decorate mat 46–7
strips of wood or plastic (fillets) 46, 47,
124

surround of frame, proportions 18
surroundings of framed picture 6
color of mats 28
"distancing" picture 28, 82
matching fabric for frame 89
wallpaper border 73

T

Tabernacle frames 122
tape 14–15
for illusion of double mat 40–1
to decorate mats 46–7
tapestry pictures, *see under* fabric
pictures
templates
stenciled designs 23
papier-mâché frames 52, 56–7
tenon saws 12–13
text (calligraphy), to be framed 120
text with pictures
double-window mats 40
family tree multi-mats 100–01
textured paper 8–9
textured surfaces (matting) 8–9, 28
three-dimensional items 105–14
butt-jointed wooden frames 72–3
mats with extra depth 36, 38–9
tiles, butt-jointed wooden frames 72–3
titles
double-window mats 40
family tree multi-mats 100–01
tools and equipment 6, 7–16, 28
accessories 16
see also specific projects
triple frames
hinged wood 98–9
medieval triptyches 122, 123
triple mats 40–1
try squares 12–13
turn clips 16

U

unglazed items 72, 82, 112–14

V

V-cut mats 42–3
varnish (glaze) 124
velvet
covering mats 36
lining box frames 106
padded frames 91
tacks 16
veneers 119, 125
visual centre of picture 28

W

wallpaper border for butt-jointed
frame 73
wash lines 44–5, 46, 125
washes on decorative mats 125
watercolor paints and brushes 14–15,
125
lines and washes 44–5, 46, 125
watercolor paper 8–9
watercolor pictures, lines and washes
on mat 44–5
wax pencils 14–15
wet mounting 124, 125
'windows' 125
windows
circular, multi-mats 100–01
double-window mats 40
oval,
fabric-covered mats 37
folded card frames 20–1
shaped (eg curve or zigzag) 68, 69–
70
wire 16

wood fillets 124
wooden frames 71–84
box frames 106–9
butt-jointed 72–3
cutout frames (birch plywood) 61–
70
cutting the glass 78–9
finishes 10, 11
liming wax 125
hinged 98–9
medieval triptyches 122, 123
miter joints 74–7, 125
slip liners 82–4
ready-made 118–9

ACKNOWLEDGMENTS

The author and publishers would like to thank the following companies for their generosity in supplying materials used in the book:
Charisma Framing
Compton Marbling
Daler Framing
Chris Longridge
Origin Framing Supplies
Photocraft (Hampstead) Ltd
K. Scharf Ltd

For the loan of artwork for framing, many thanks are due to:
Chloe Alexander
Belmont Middle School
Aurelio Campa
Diana Dawson
Devonshire House School
Caroline Frank
Jacqueline Frank
Belinda Harding
Hazel Harrison
Andrea Lyttleton
Ben Lyttleton
Jonathan Lyttleton
Binnie and Nigel Manger
Frances Pennington
Sylvia Pepper
Judith Simons
Henrietta Wilkinson

The author and publishers would also like to thank Martin Stubbings of Charisma Framing for invaluable advice and assistance, Diana Thomson for creative assistance, Diana Dawson for decorative fabric frames, Marion Elliott for papier-mâché frames and Peter Frank for general assistance and support.

The author and publishers acknowledge copyright of the following material: origami frame design on pages 24 and 25 by Florence Temko, author of *Paper Pandas and Jumping Frogs* published by China Books and Periodicals, San Francisco Athena International for postcards and prints, featured on pages 18, 46–47, 66–67, 69, 98–99, 102–103.